Lenny's Lavvu Adventure

written by

Sylva Fae

COPYRIGHT

Text ©2024 copyright @ Sylva Fae.
Illustrations sourced and purchased from various royalty free websites.

First published in the UK in April 2024

DEDICATION

To John Kelenfoldi, whose idea it was to write a story about a Lavvu, and to all my Lavvu buddies – happy camping!

Sylva Fae

To my beautiful late wife, Lorna, and my dear friend, Agnieszka Boratynska, who got me my first Lavvu – kindest regards.

John Kelenfoldi

ALSO BY SYLVA FAE

Rainbow Monsters - Winner of Chanticleer Little Peeps Award
Mindful Monsters - Finalist in Chanticleer Little Peeps Awards
Rainbow Monsters Colouring Fun
Children's Christmas Collection – 4 book boxset
No Place Like Home
Yoga Fox - Winner of Chanticleer Award and Reader's Choice Award
Bea & Bee - Overall winner of Reader's Choice Awards
Elfabet - Winner of Chanticleer Little Peeps Award
The Shimmer - Reader's Choice Award
That Pesky Pixie - Reader's Choice Award
I Can Be Anything – Girl and Boy editions
Secret Santas
Messy Christmas
The Littlest Owl's Christmas Rescue
Halloween Parade
Spooky Spells – StoryPuzzle
Autumn Fall – StoryPuzzle
Woodland Warriors – Winner of Reader's Choice Award
Time to Shine – Overall winner of Reader's Choice Award
Tall Tree Tales

Hello! My name is Lenny,

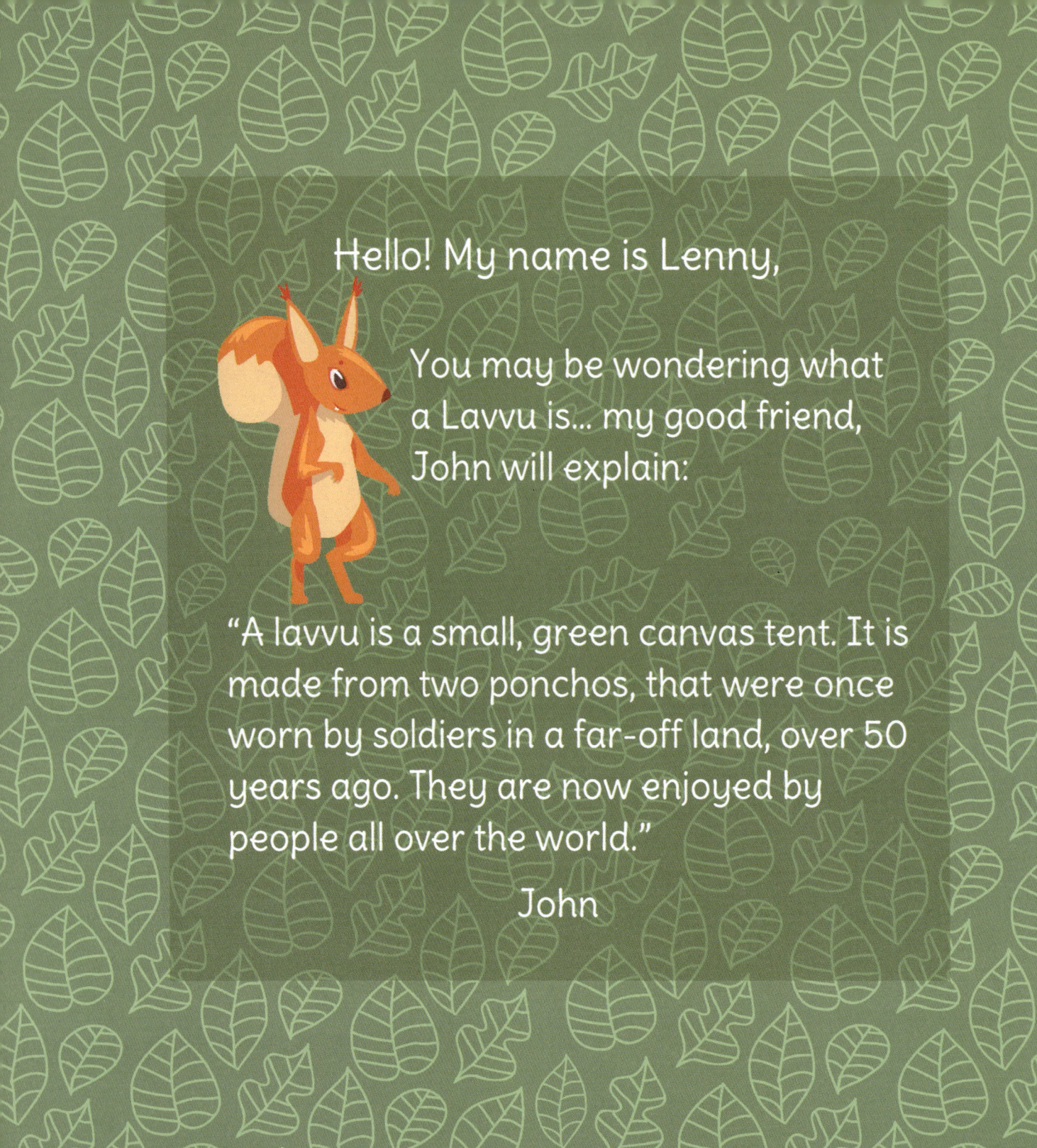

You may be wondering what a Lavvu is... my good friend, John will explain:

"A lavvu is a small, green canvas tent. It is made from two ponchos, that were once worn by soldiers in a far-off land, over 50 years ago. They are now enjoyed by people all over the world."

John

You can fasten the two ponchos together to make a small tent.

Once upon a time,
in a green forest glade,
lived Lenny the squirrel;
he was curious and brave.

He played in the trees,
but soon grew quite bored.
He yearned for adventure,
to run and explore.

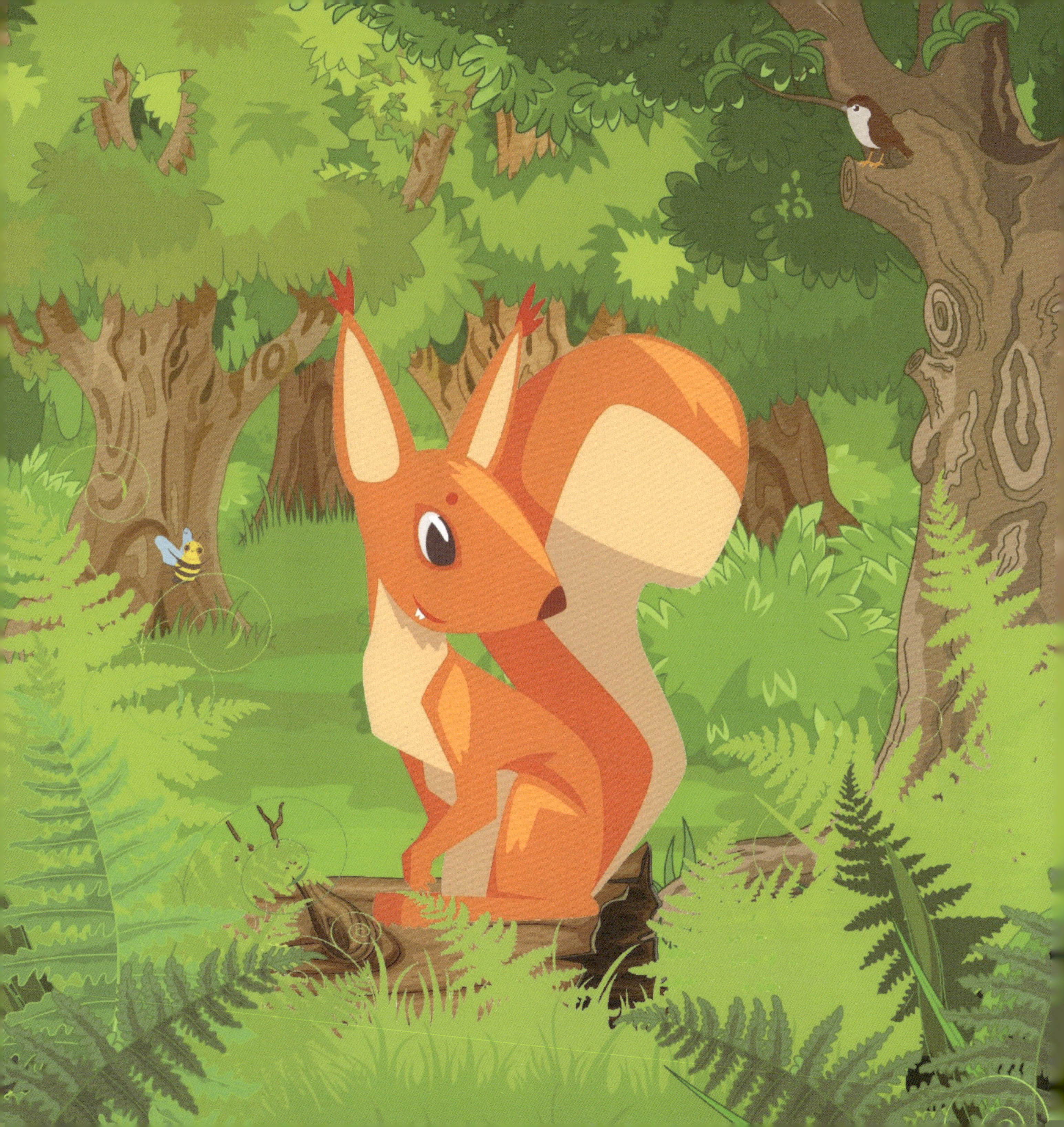

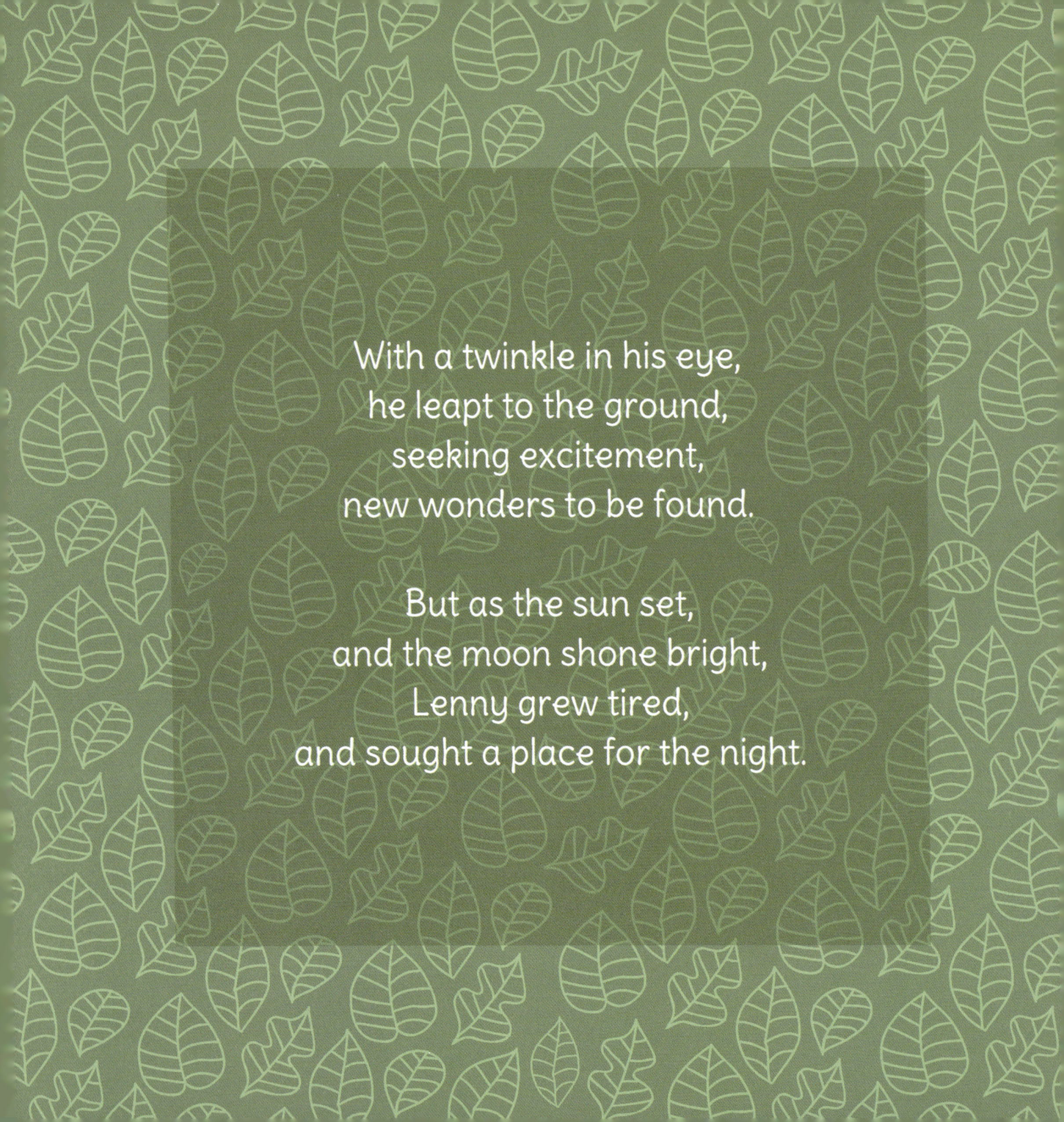

With a twinkle in his eye,
he leapt to the ground,
seeking excitement,
new wonders to be found.

But as the sun set,
and the moon shone bright,
Lenny grew tired,
and sought a place for the night.

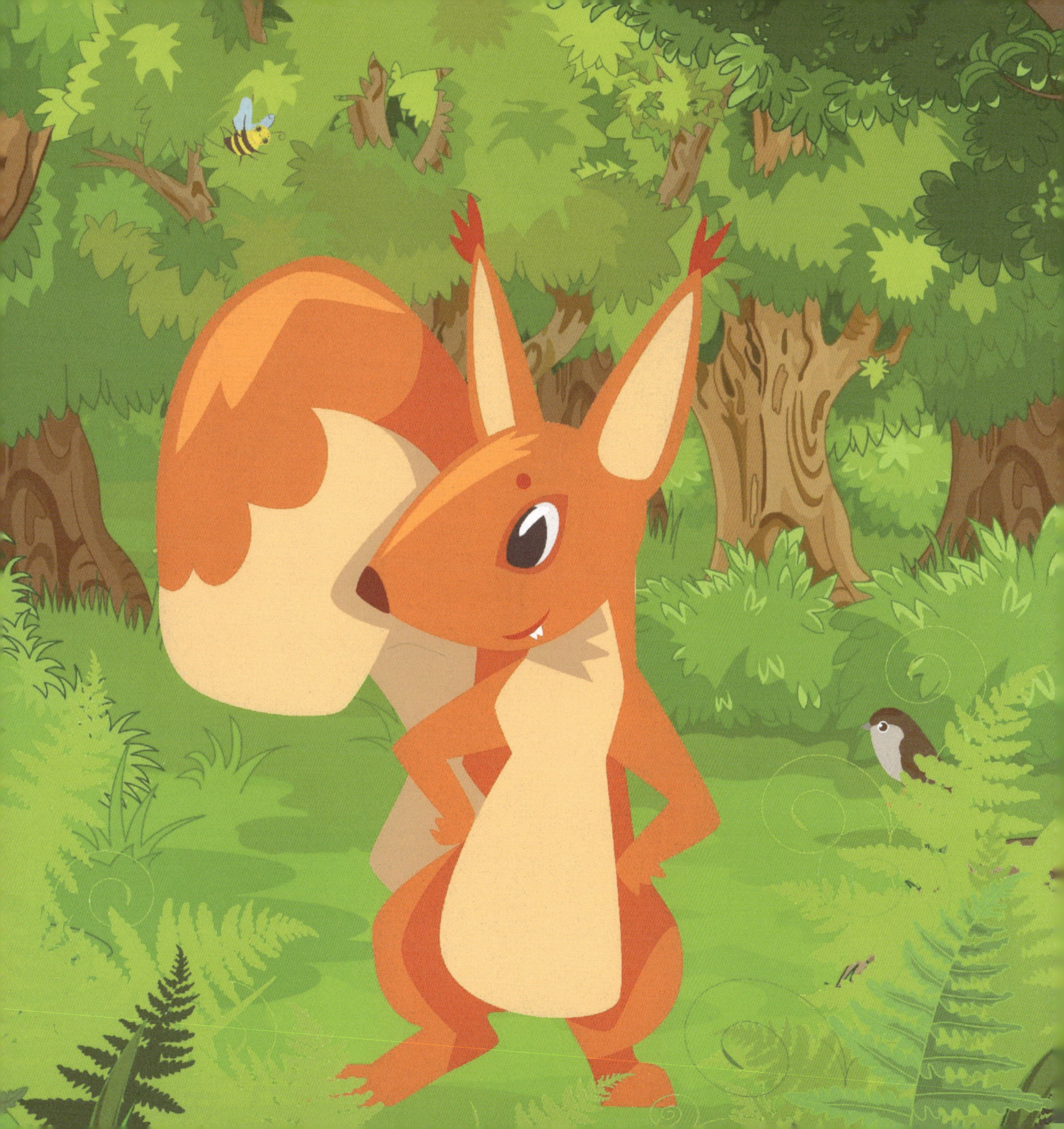

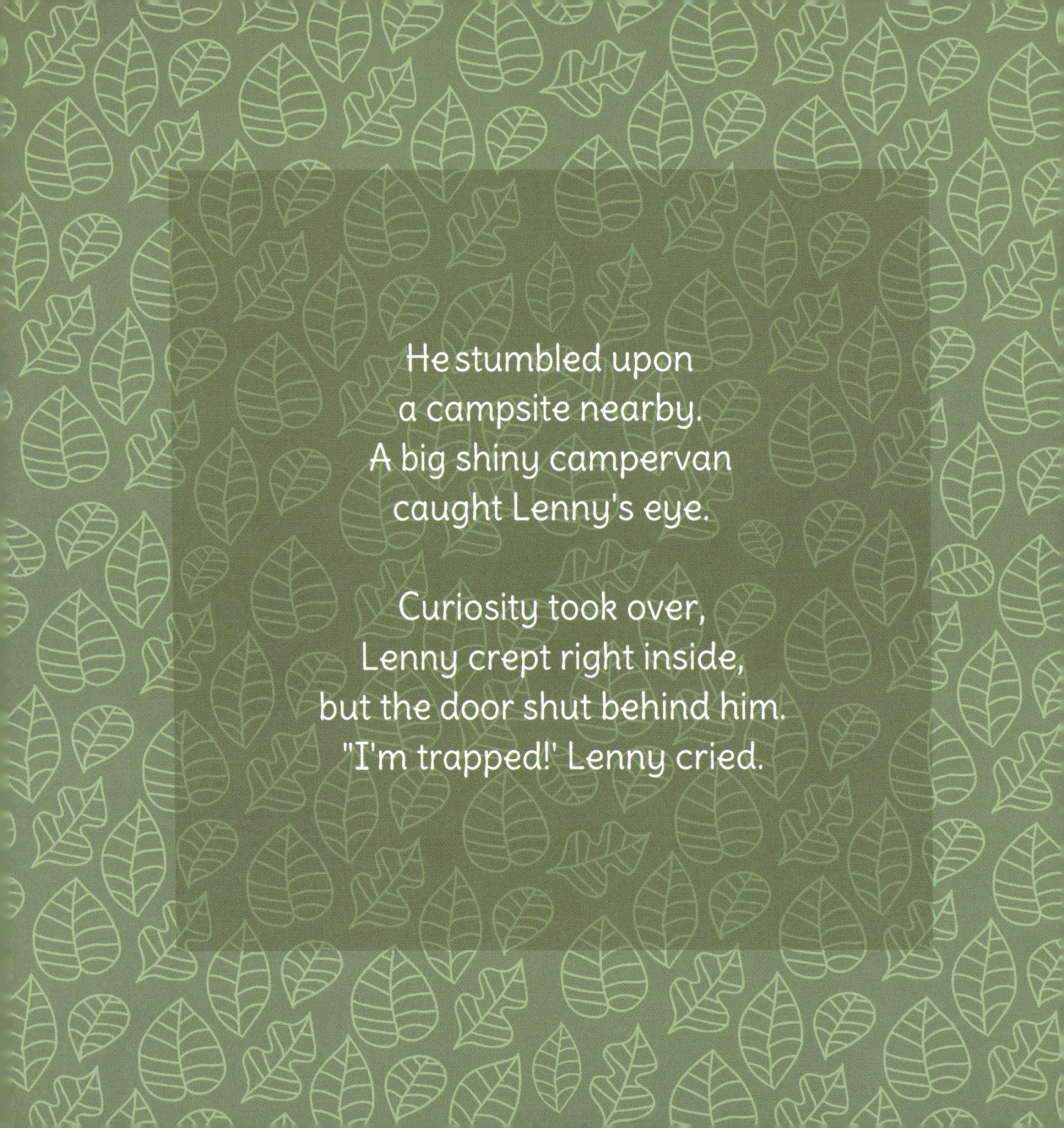

He stumbled upon
a campsite nearby.
A big shiny campervan
caught Lenny's eye.

Curiosity took over,
Lenny crept right inside,
but the door shut behind him.
"I'm trapped!' Lenny cried.

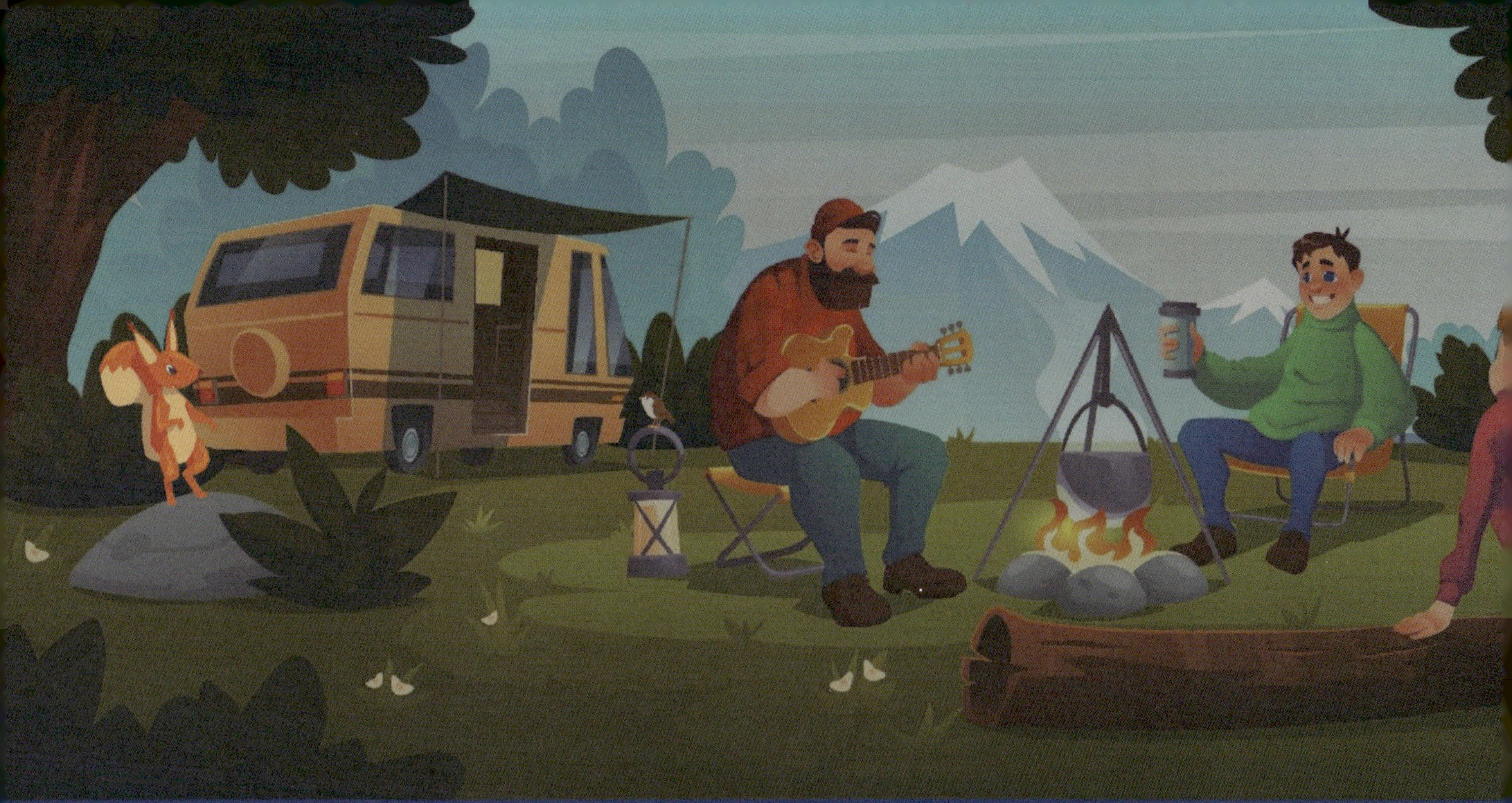

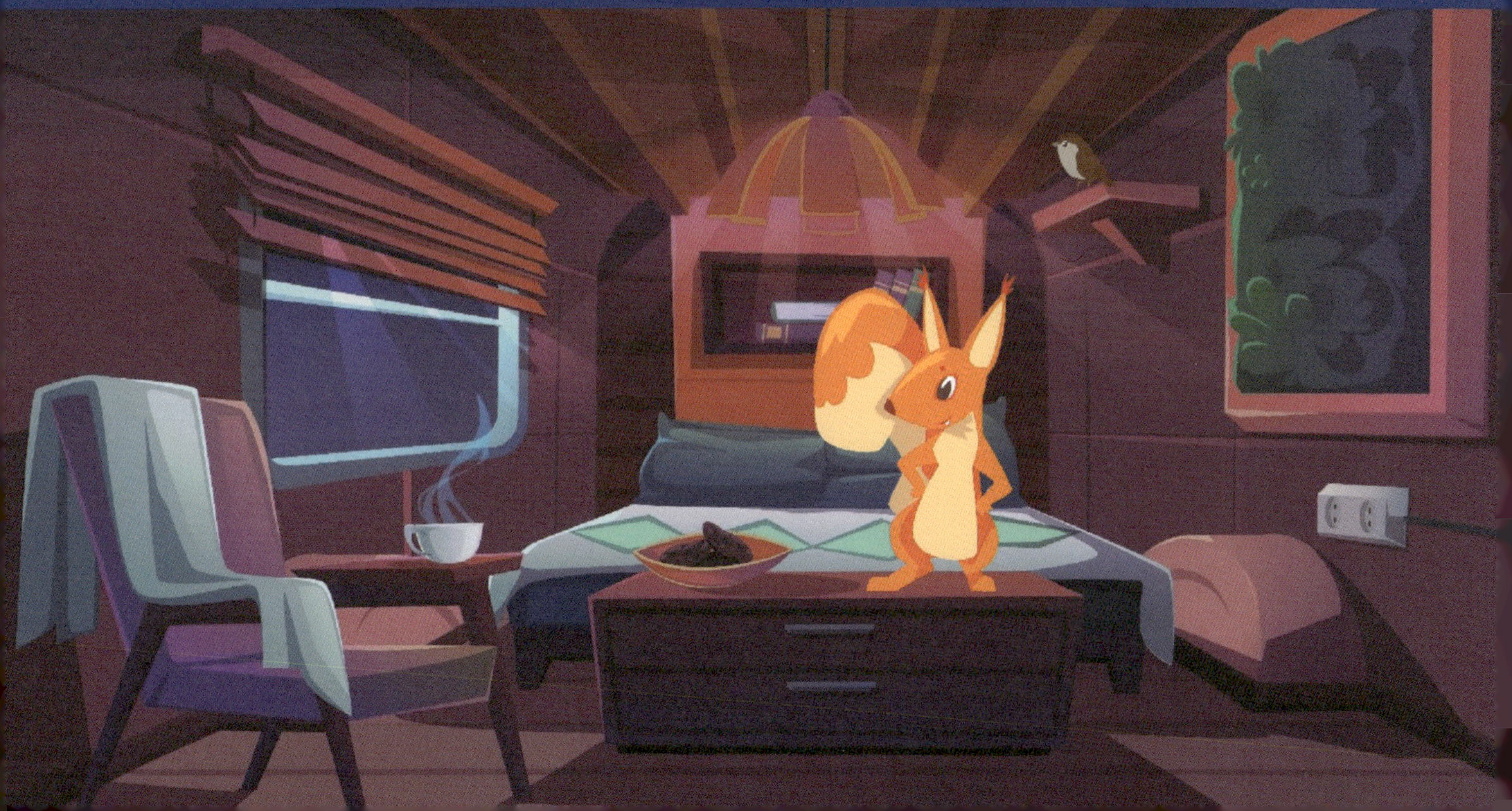

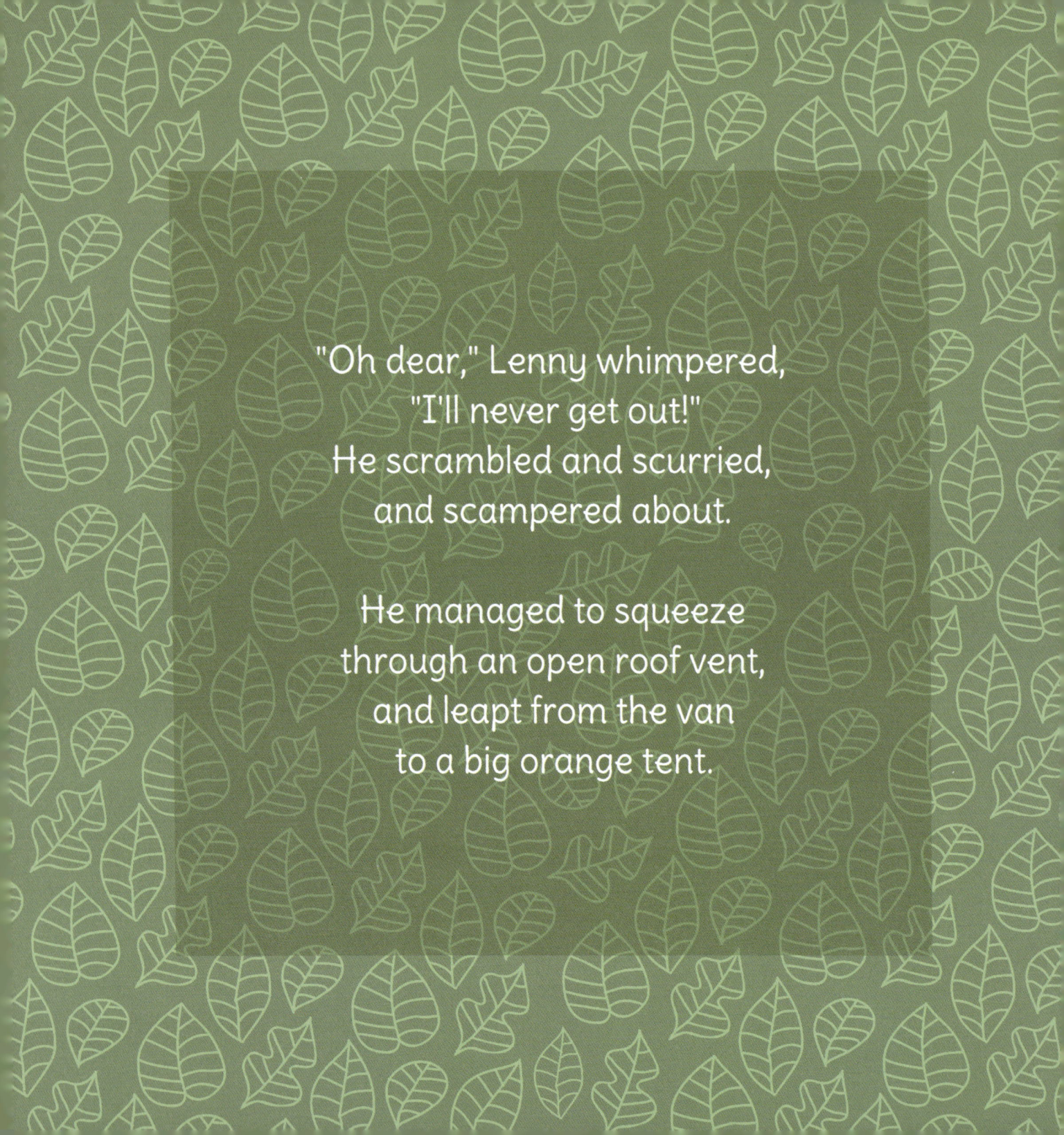

"Oh dear," Lenny whimpered,
"I'll never get out!"
He scrambled and scurried,
and scampered about.

He managed to squeeze
through an open roof vent,
and leapt from the van
to a big orange tent.

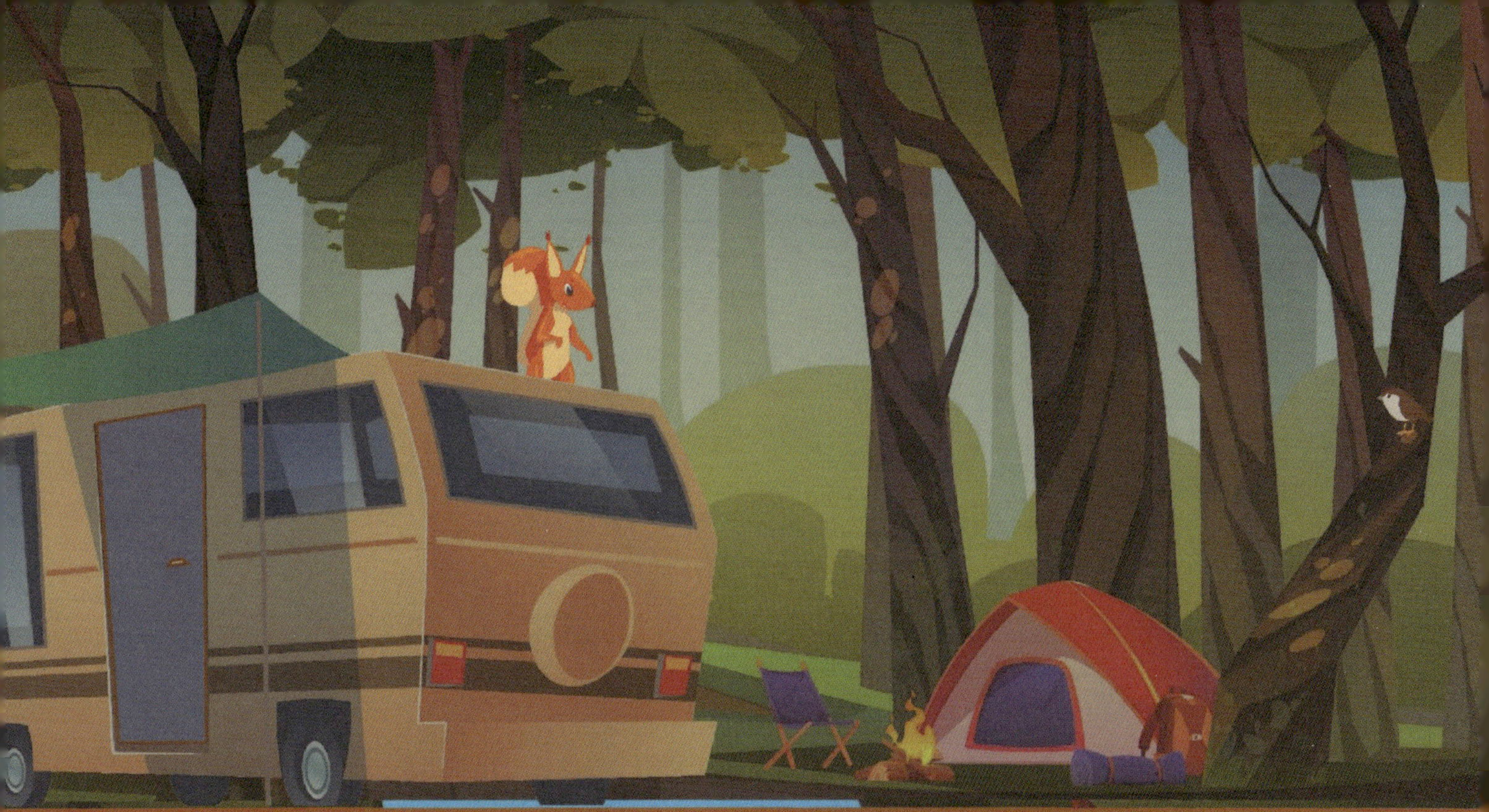

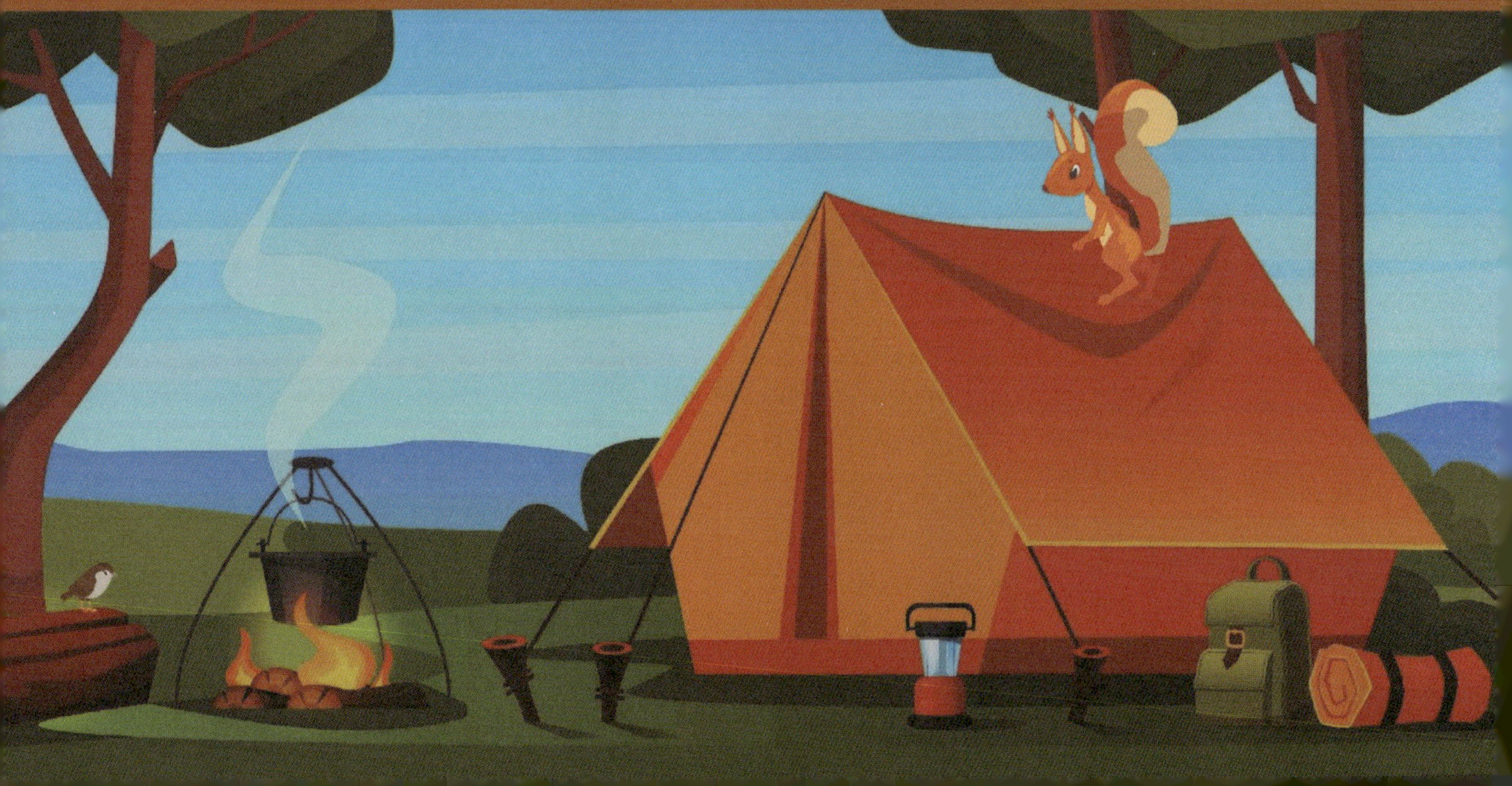

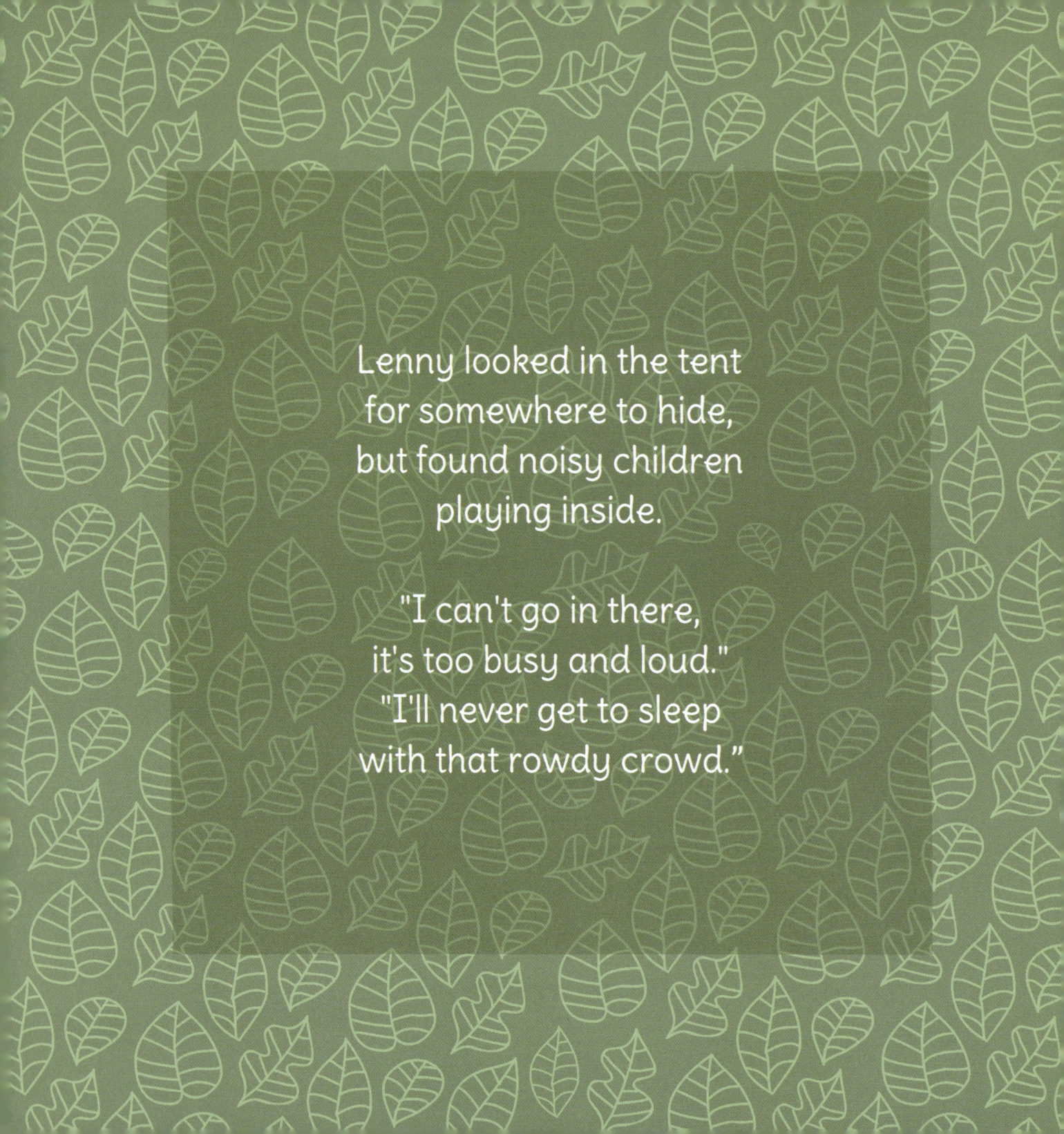

Lenny looked in the tent
for somewhere to hide,
but found noisy children
playing inside.

"I can't go in there,
it's too busy and loud."
"I'll never get to sleep
with that rowdy crowd."

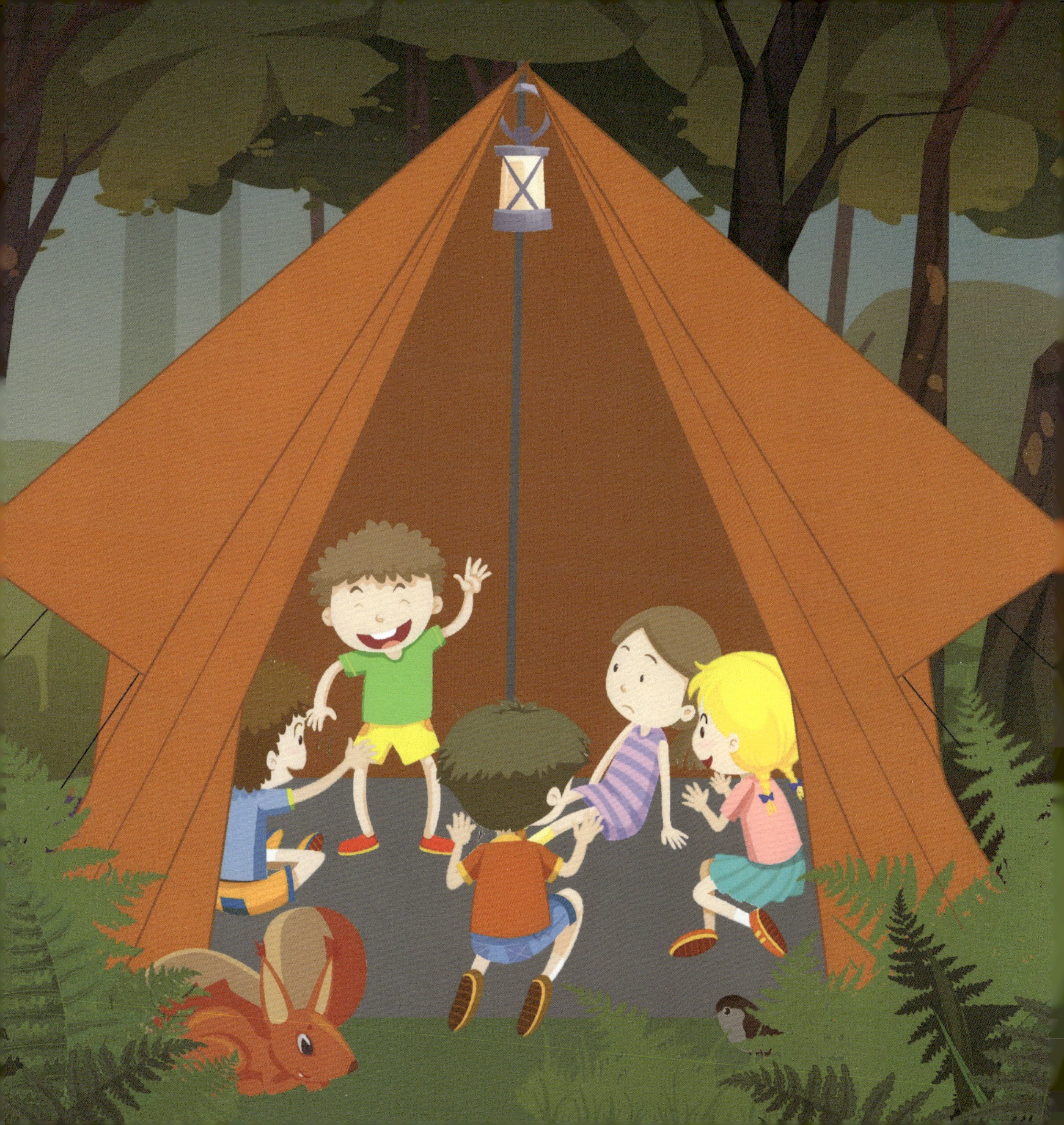

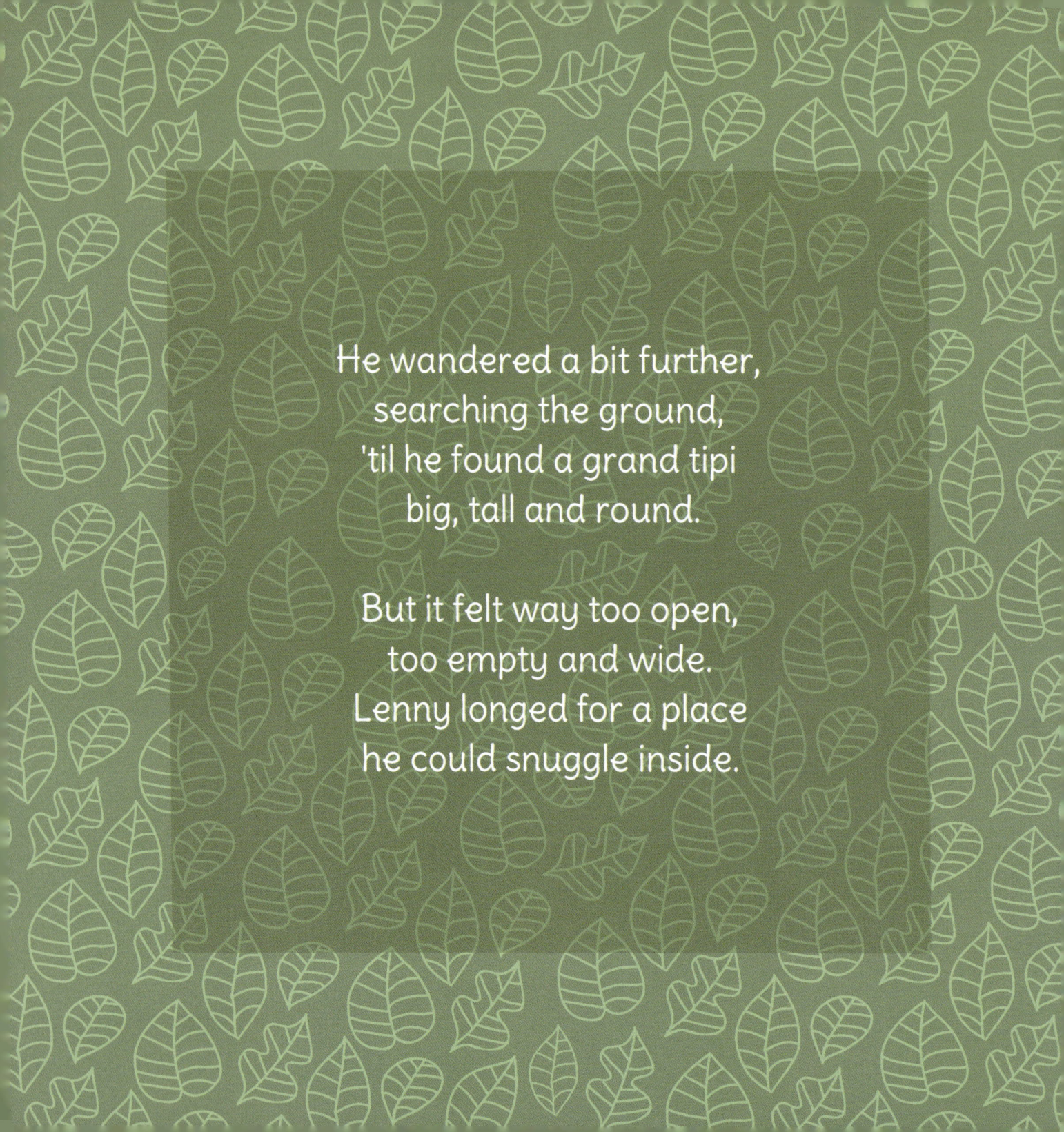

He wandered a bit further,
searching the ground,
'til he found a grand tipi
big, tall and round.

But it felt way too open,
too empty and wide.
Lenny longed for a place
he could snuggle inside.

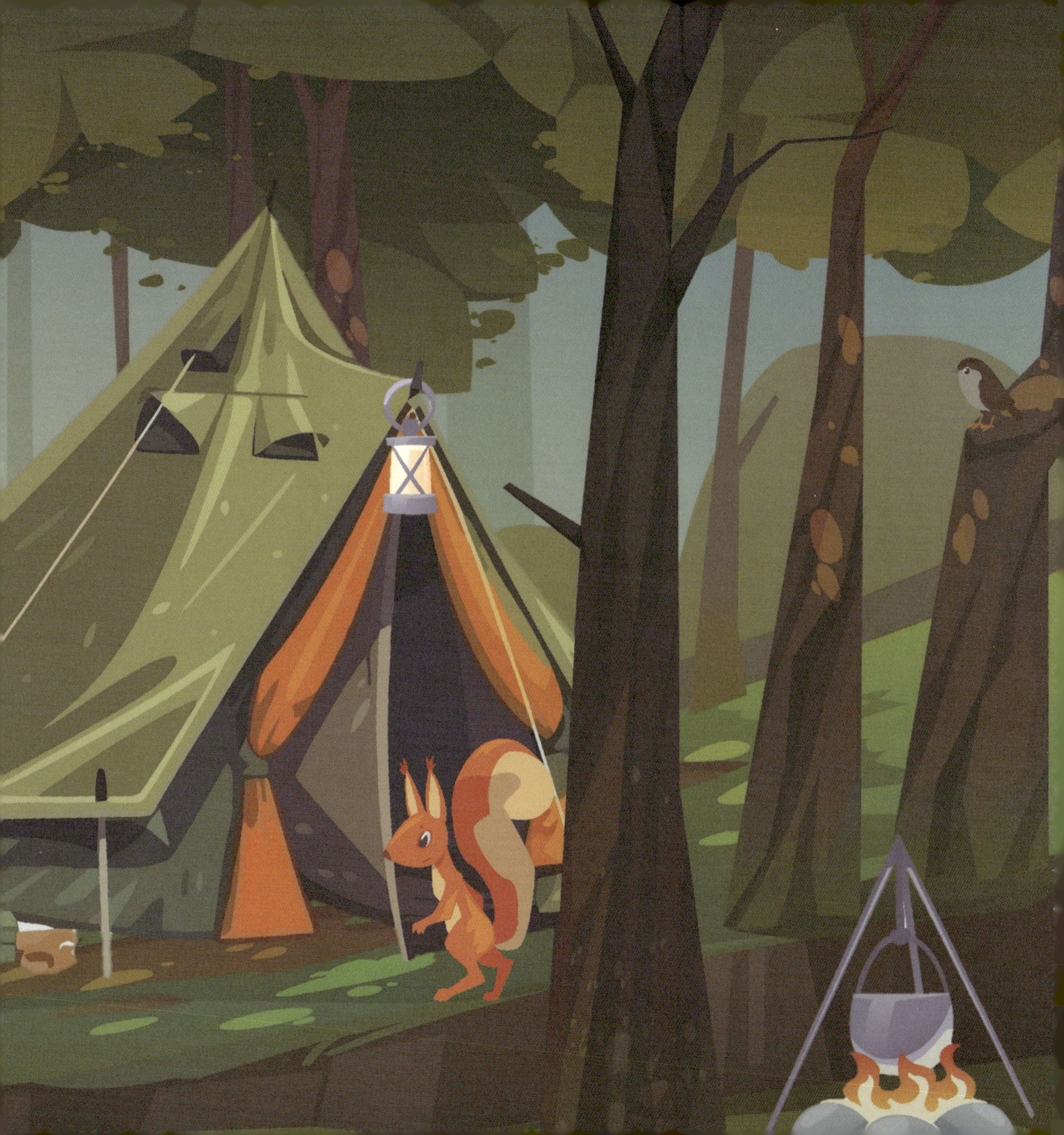

Weary and tired,
he searched through the site,
for a cozy bed
that was peaceful and right.

Lenny trudged on,
shivering in the cool breeze,
then he spotted a Lavvu
hidden deep in the trees.

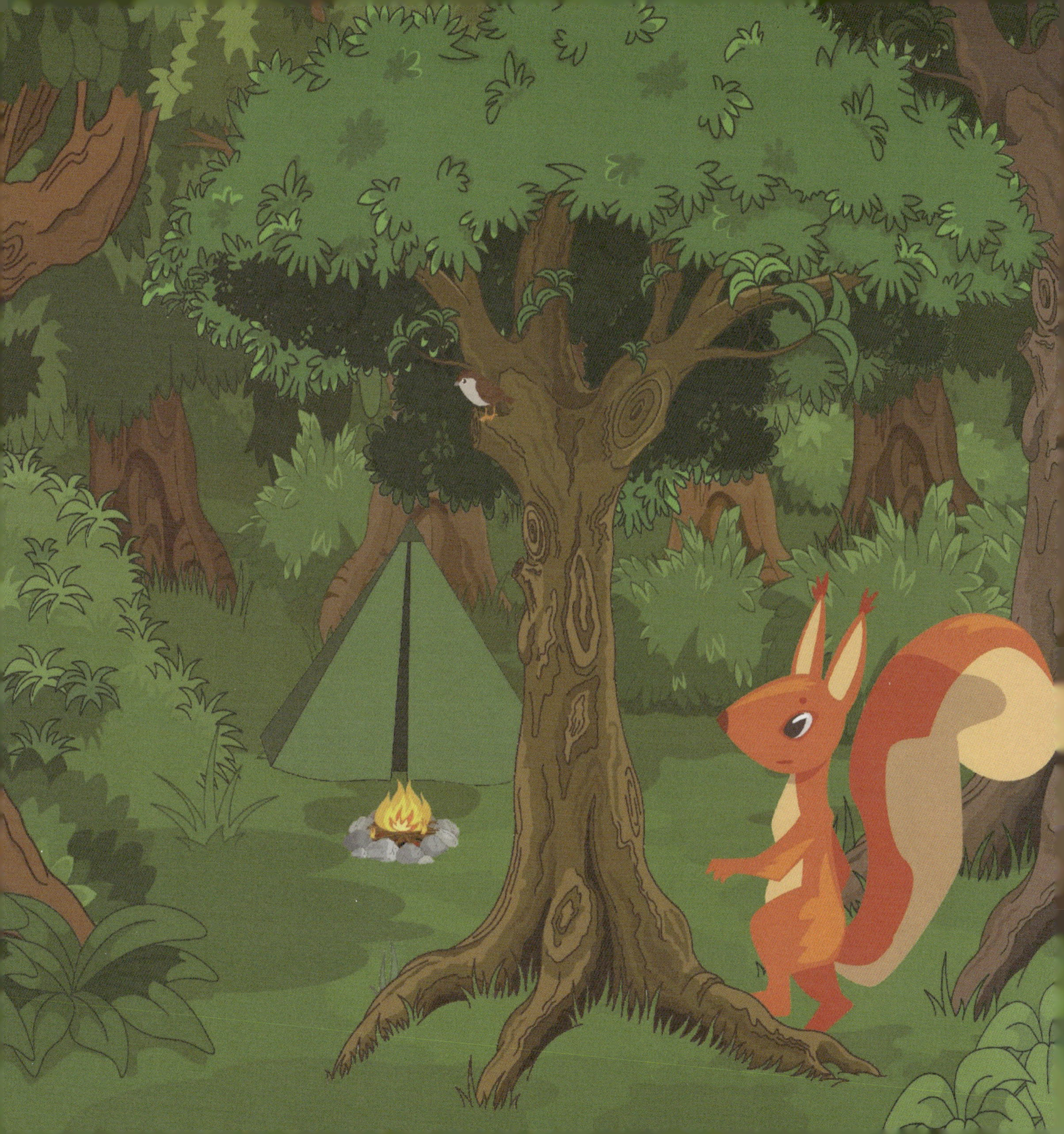

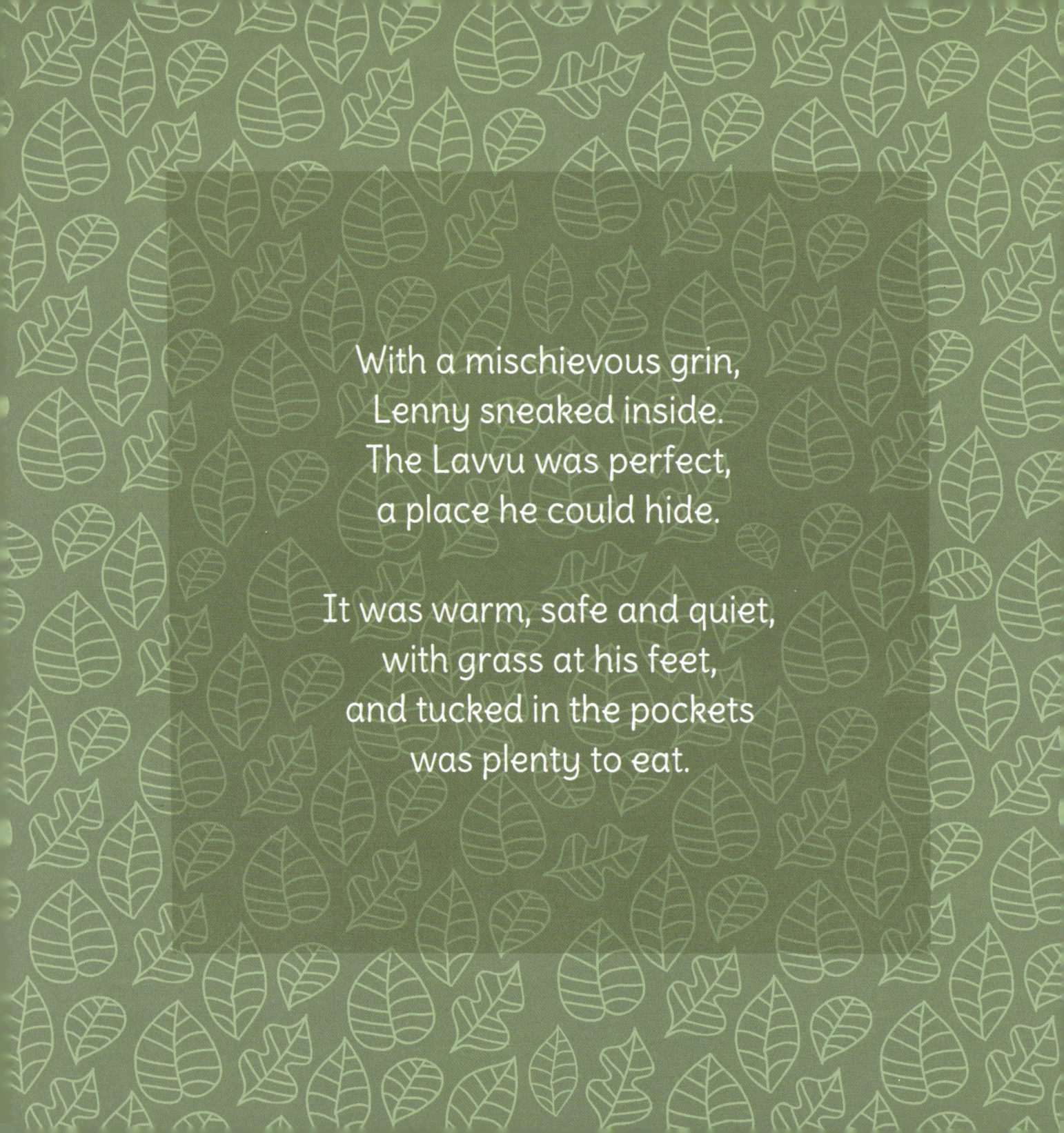

With a mischievous grin,
Lenny sneaked inside.
The Lavvu was perfect,
a place he could hide.

It was warm, safe and quiet,
with grass at his feet,
and tucked in the pockets
was plenty to eat.

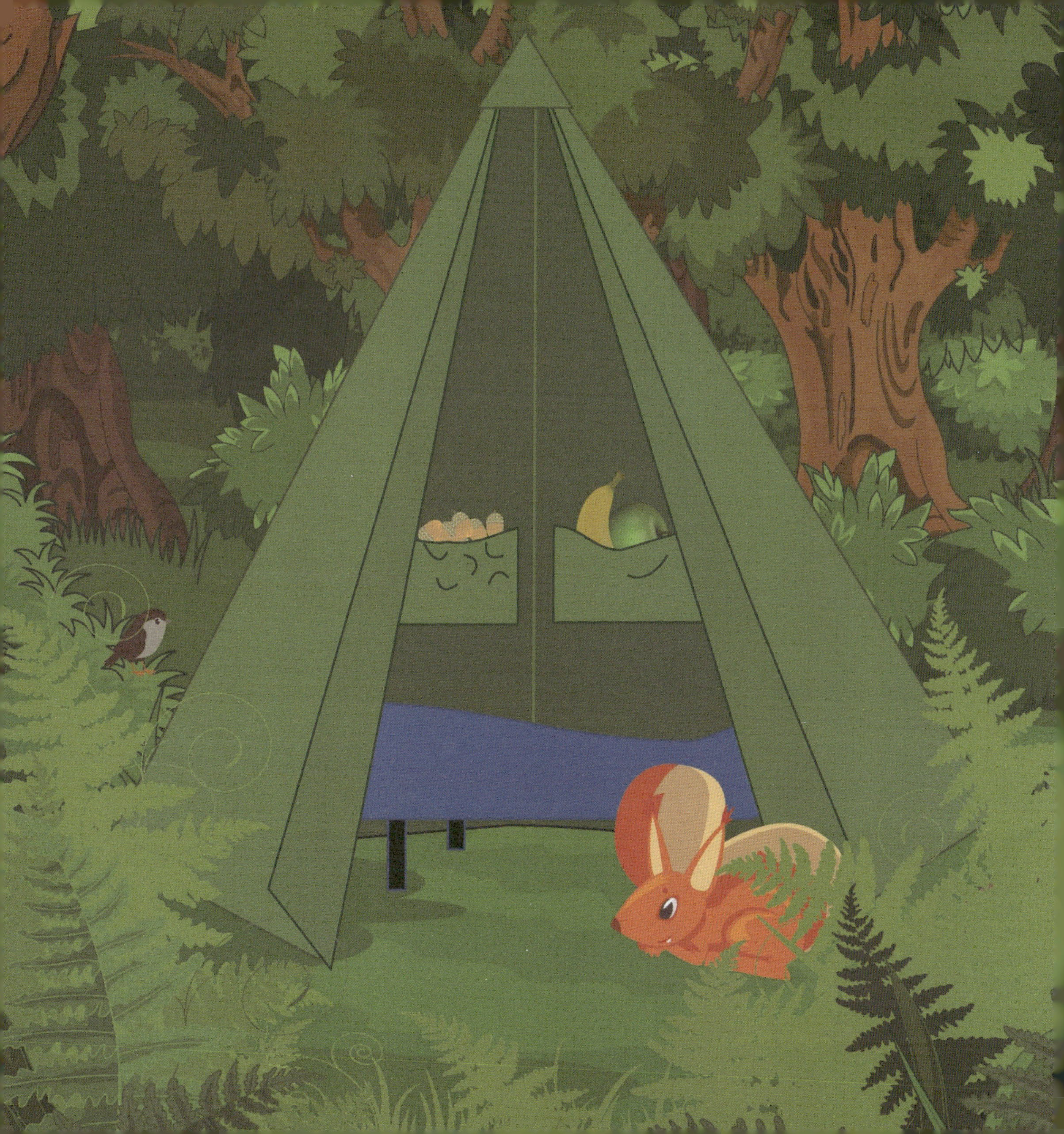

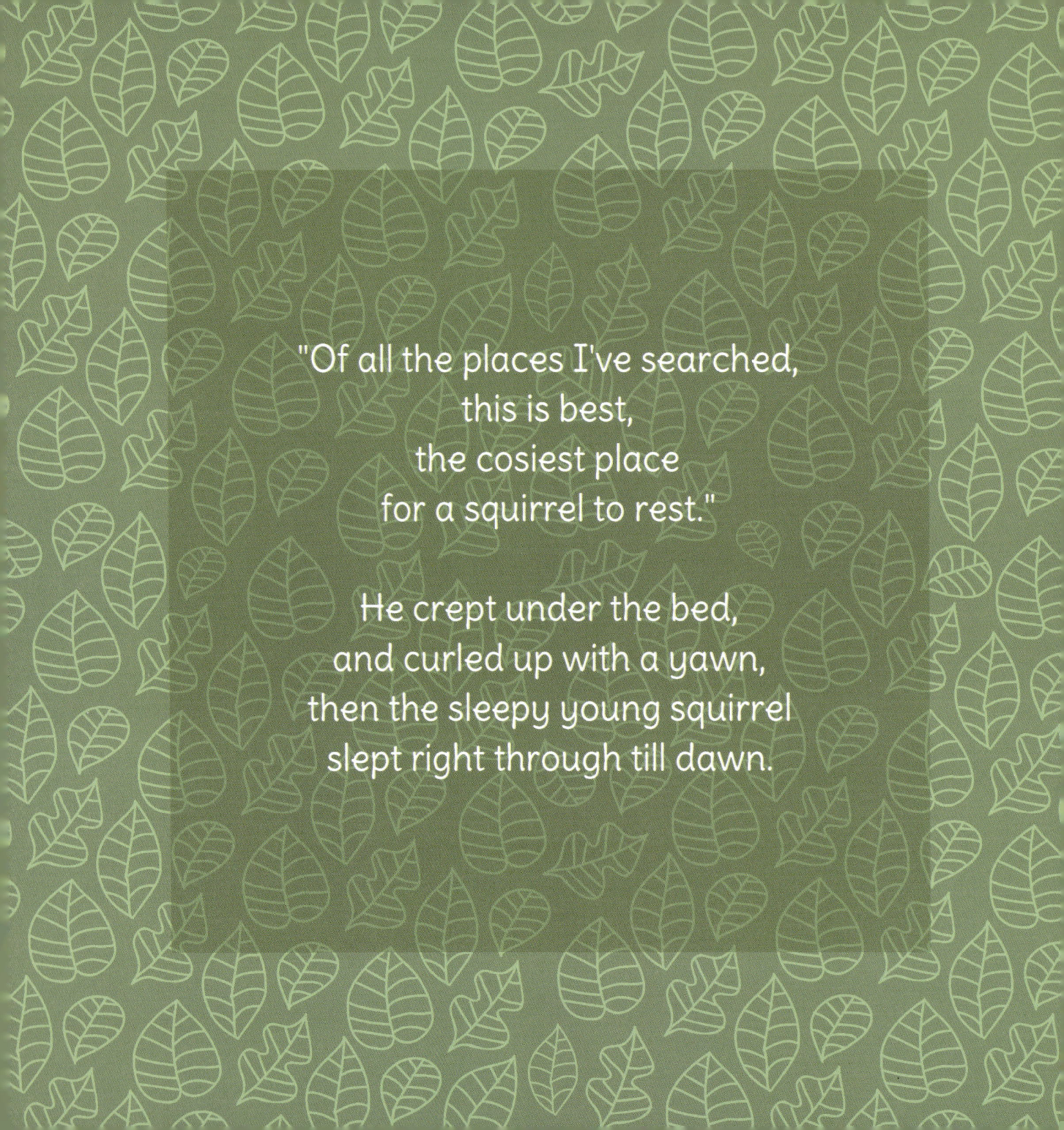

"Of all the places I've searched,
this is best,
the cosiest place
for a squirrel to rest."

He crept under the bed,
and curled up with a yawn,
then the sleepy young squirrel
slept right through till dawn.

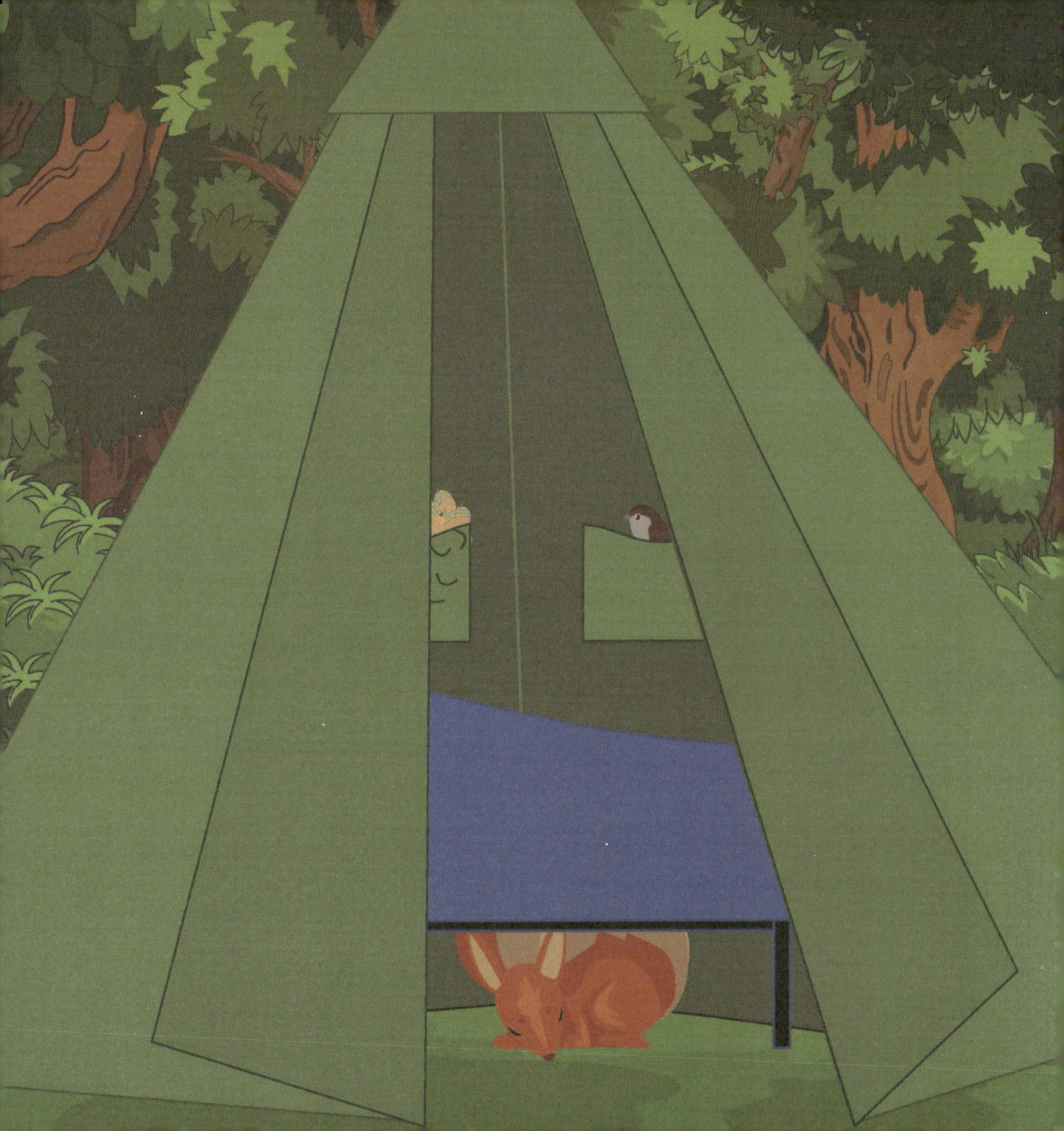

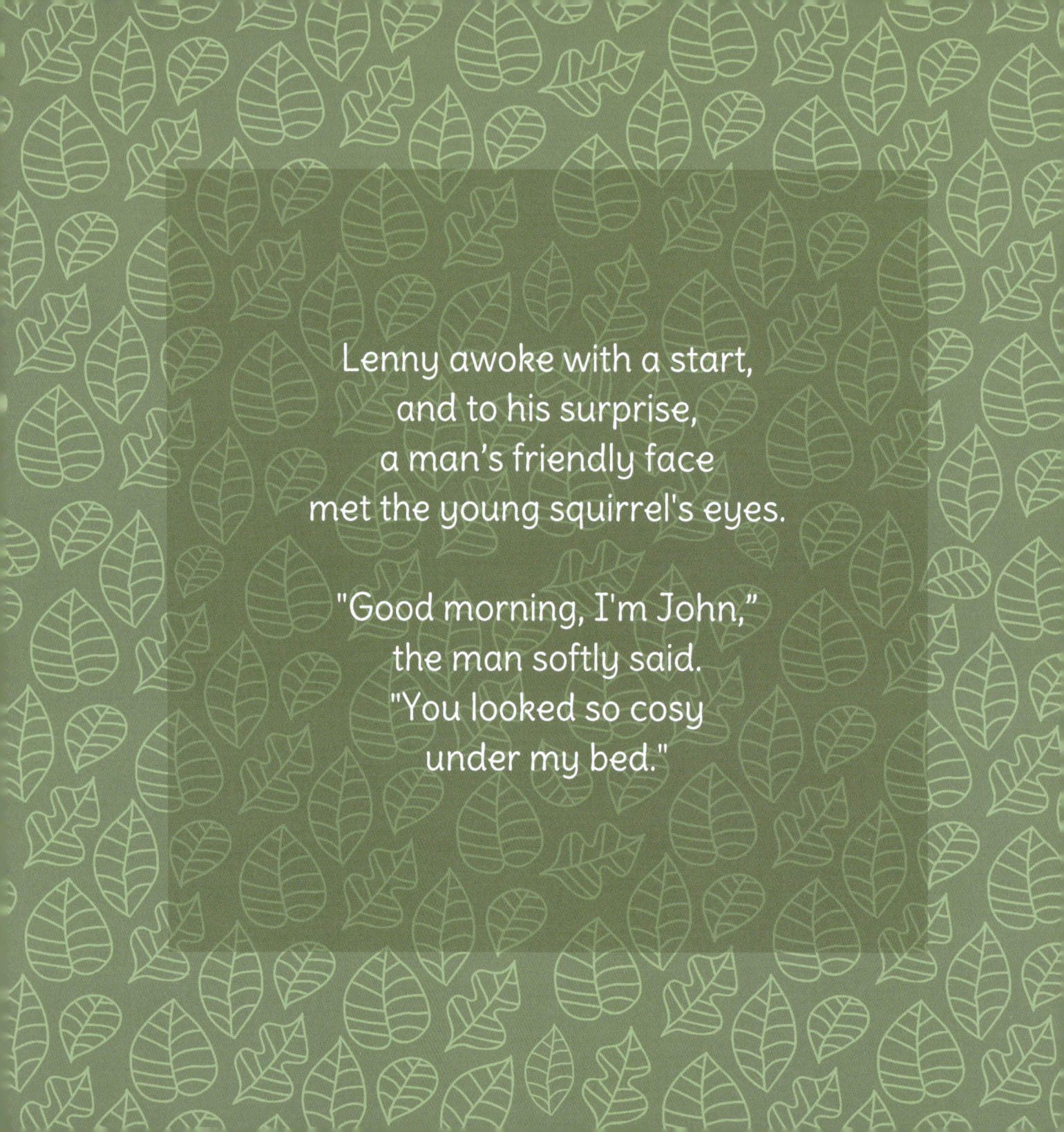

Lenny awoke with a start,
and to his surprise,
a man's friendly face
met the young squirrel's eyes.

"Good morning, I'm John,"
the man softly said.
"You looked so cosy
under my bed."

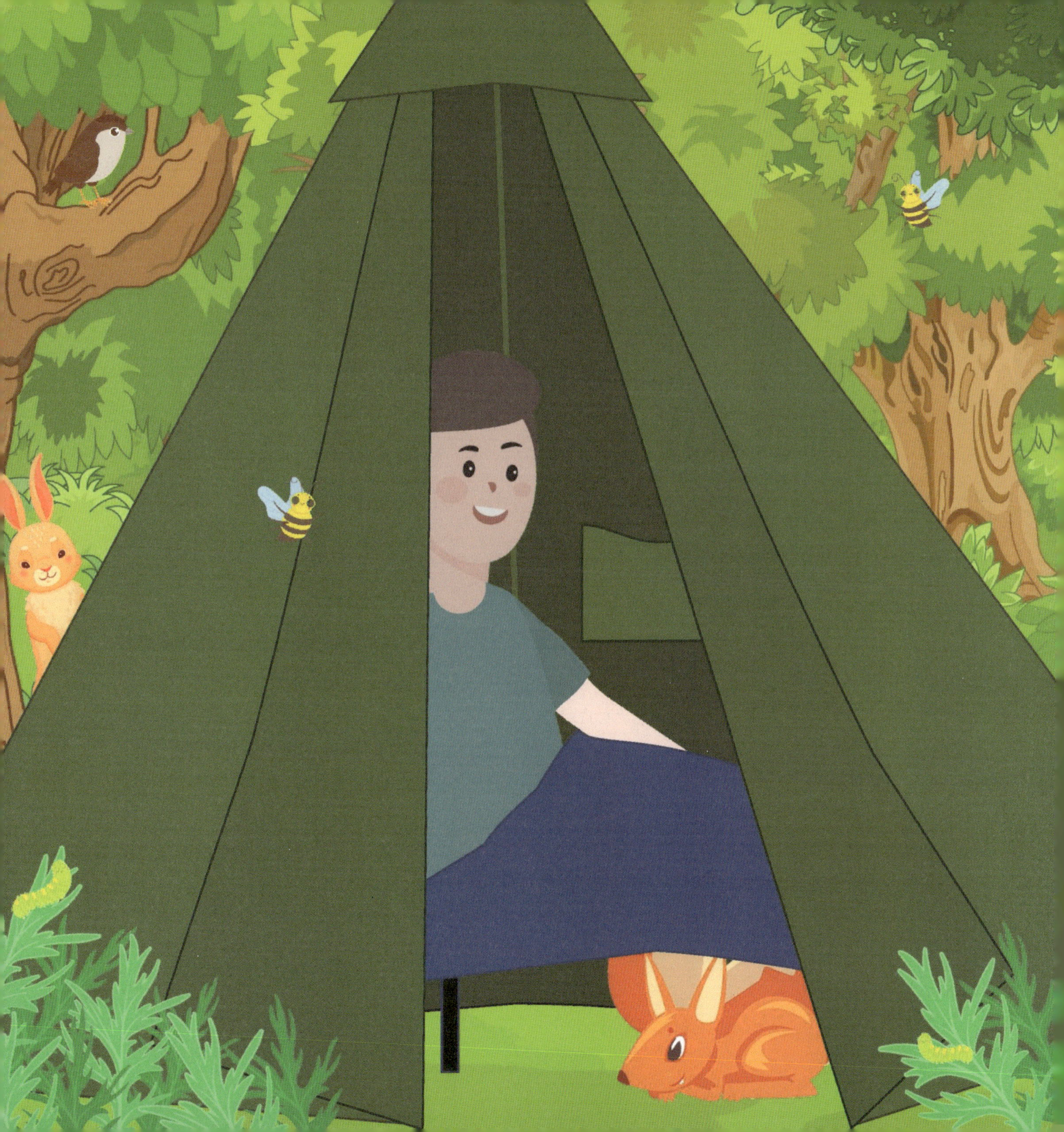

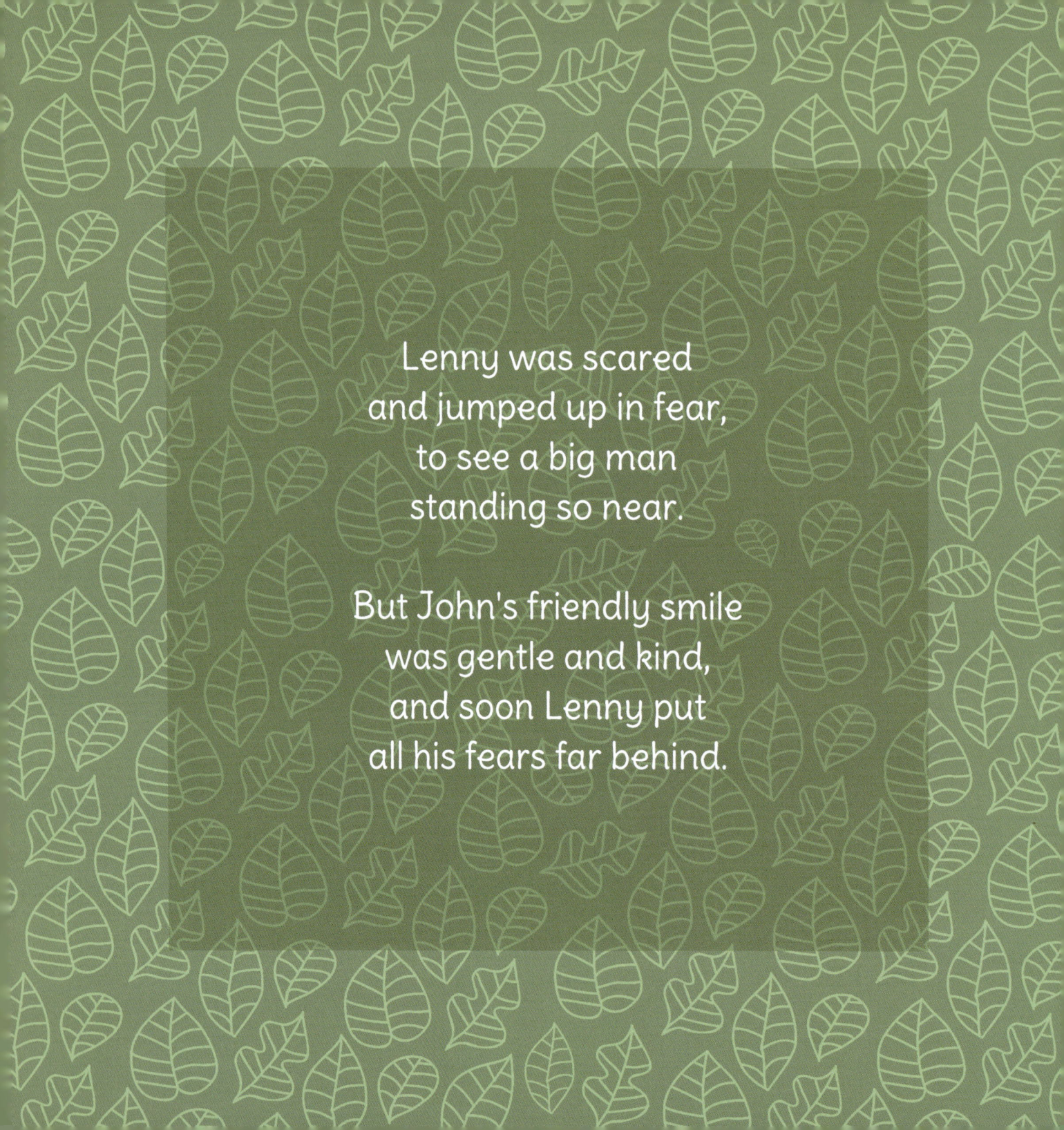

Lenny was scared
and jumped up in fear,
to see a big man
standing so near.

But John's friendly smile
was gentle and kind,
and soon Lenny put
all his fears far behind.

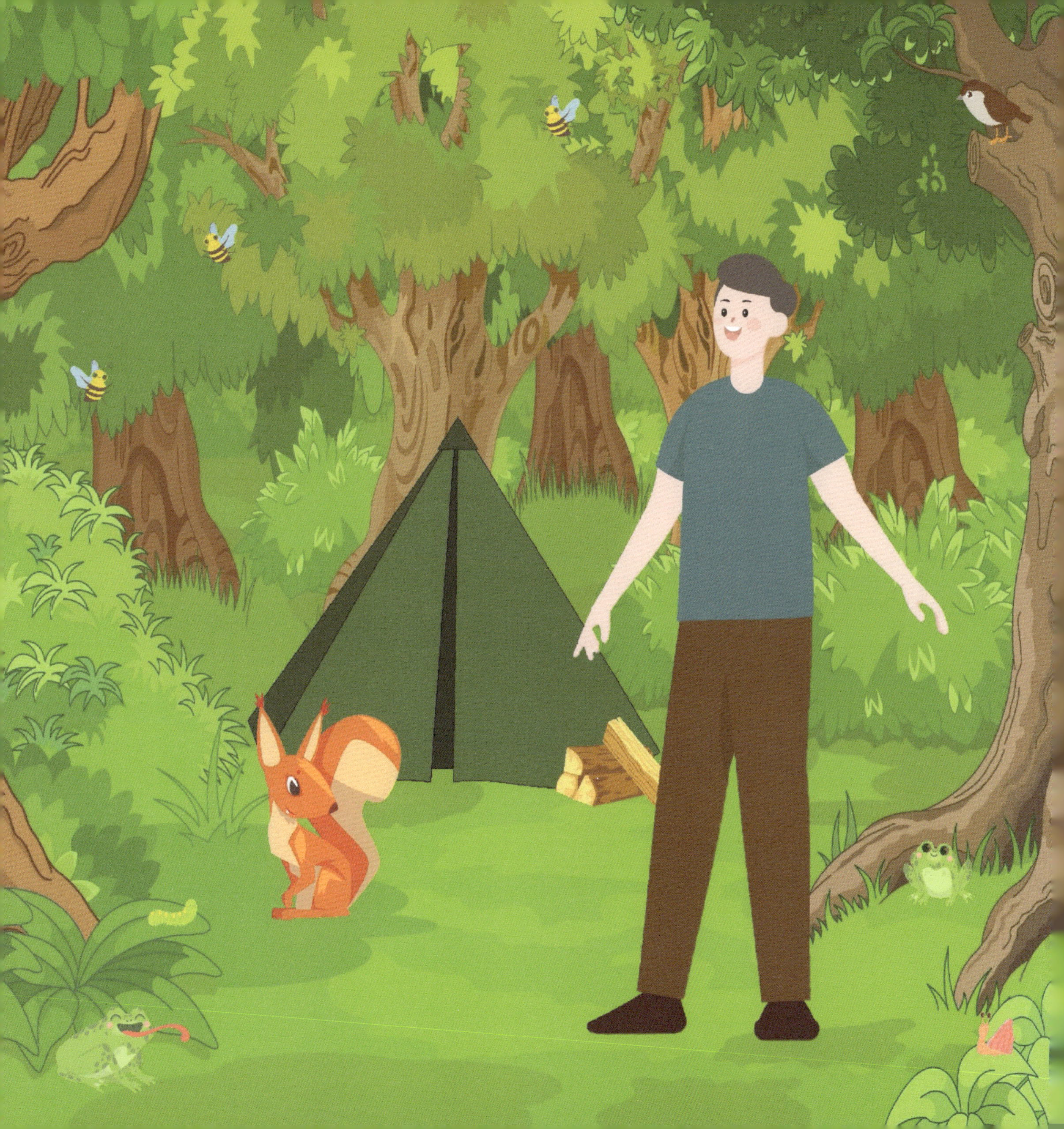

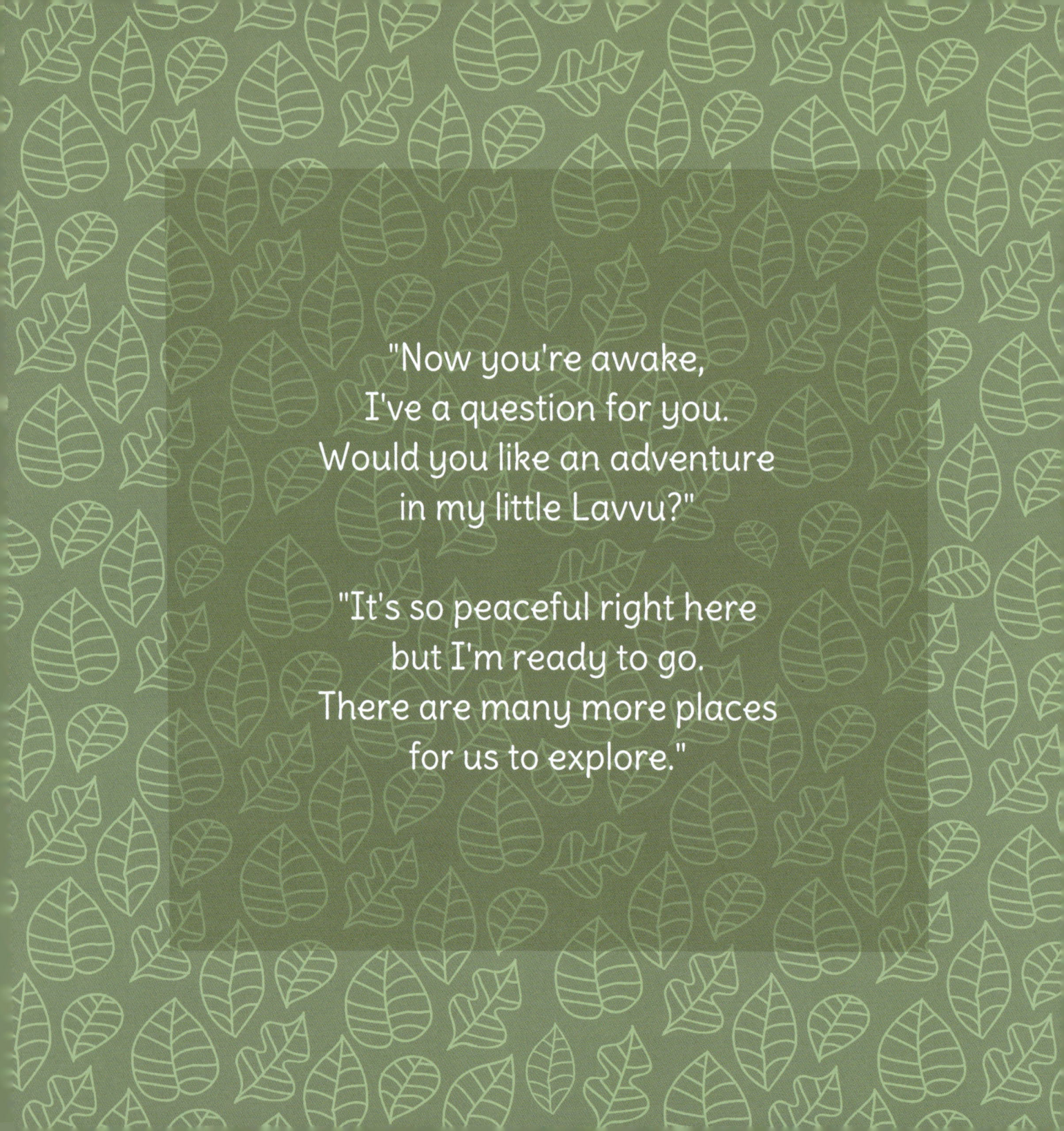

"Now you're awake,
I've a question for you.
Would you like an adventure
in my little Lavvu?"

"It's so peaceful right here
but I'm ready to go.
There are many more places
for us to explore."

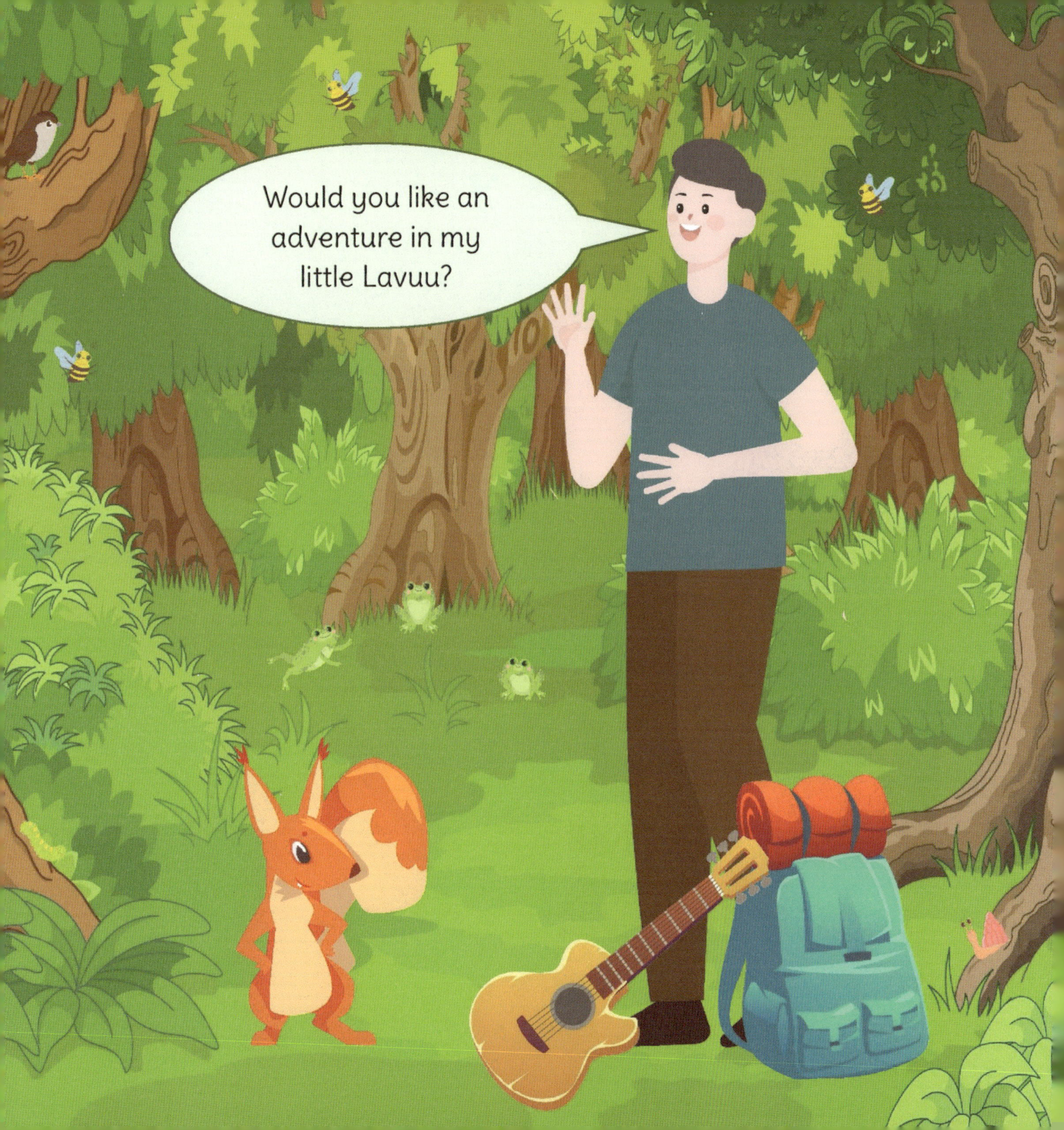
Would you like an adventure in my little Lavuu?

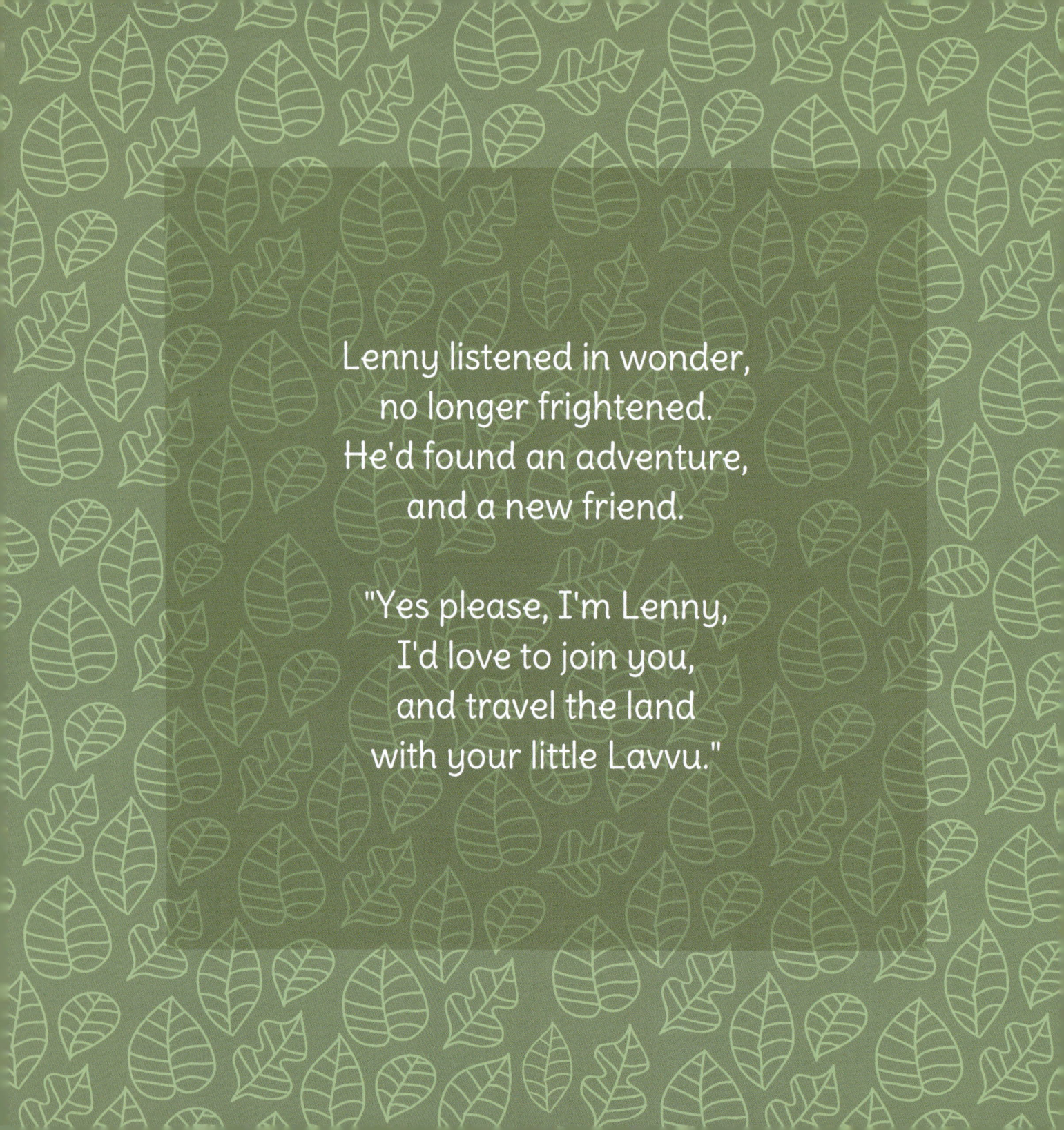

Lenny listened in wonder,
no longer frightened.
He'd found an adventure,
and a new friend.

"Yes please, I'm Lenny,
I'd love to join you,
and travel the land
with your little Lavvu."

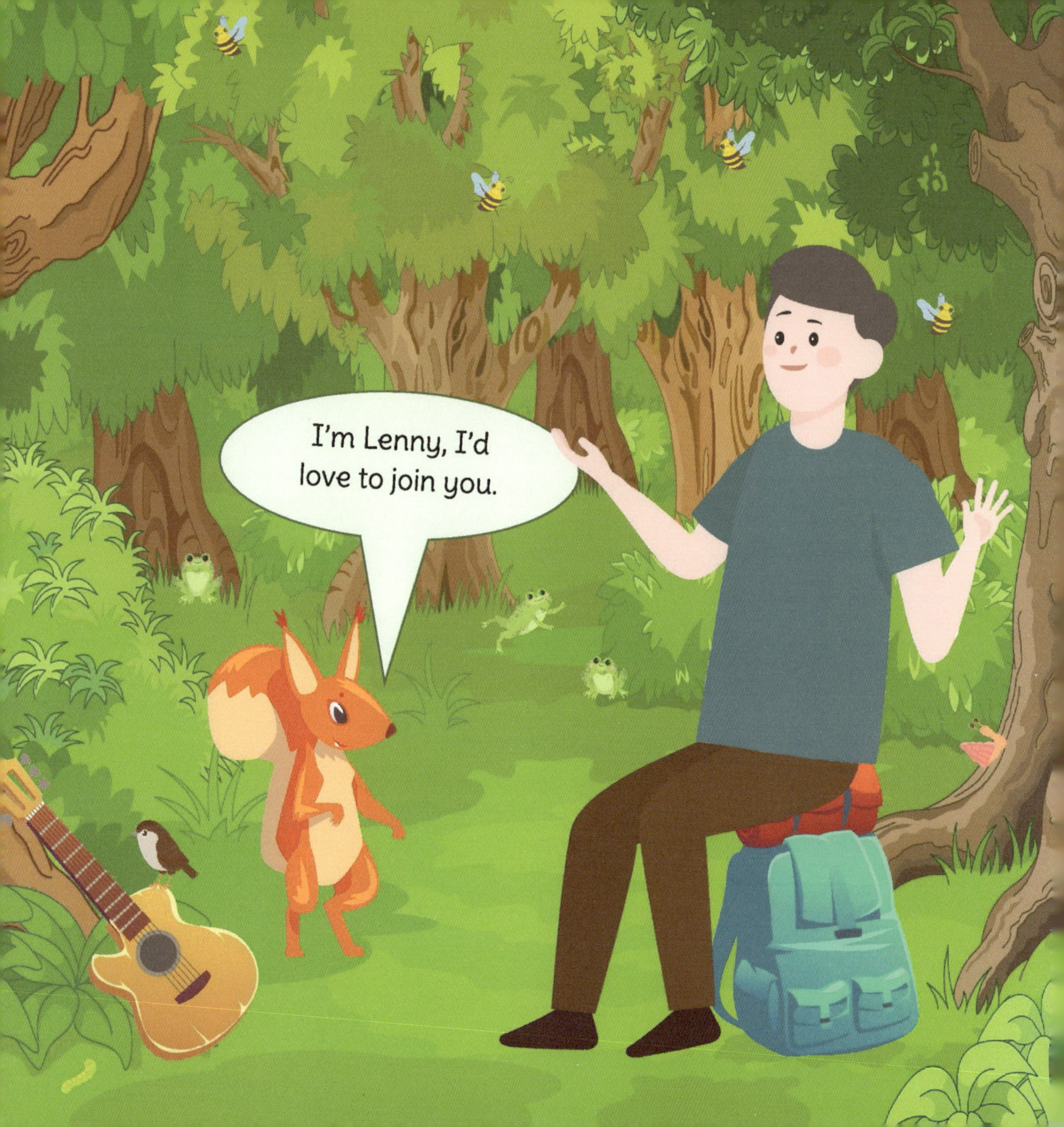
I'm Lenny, I'd love to join you.

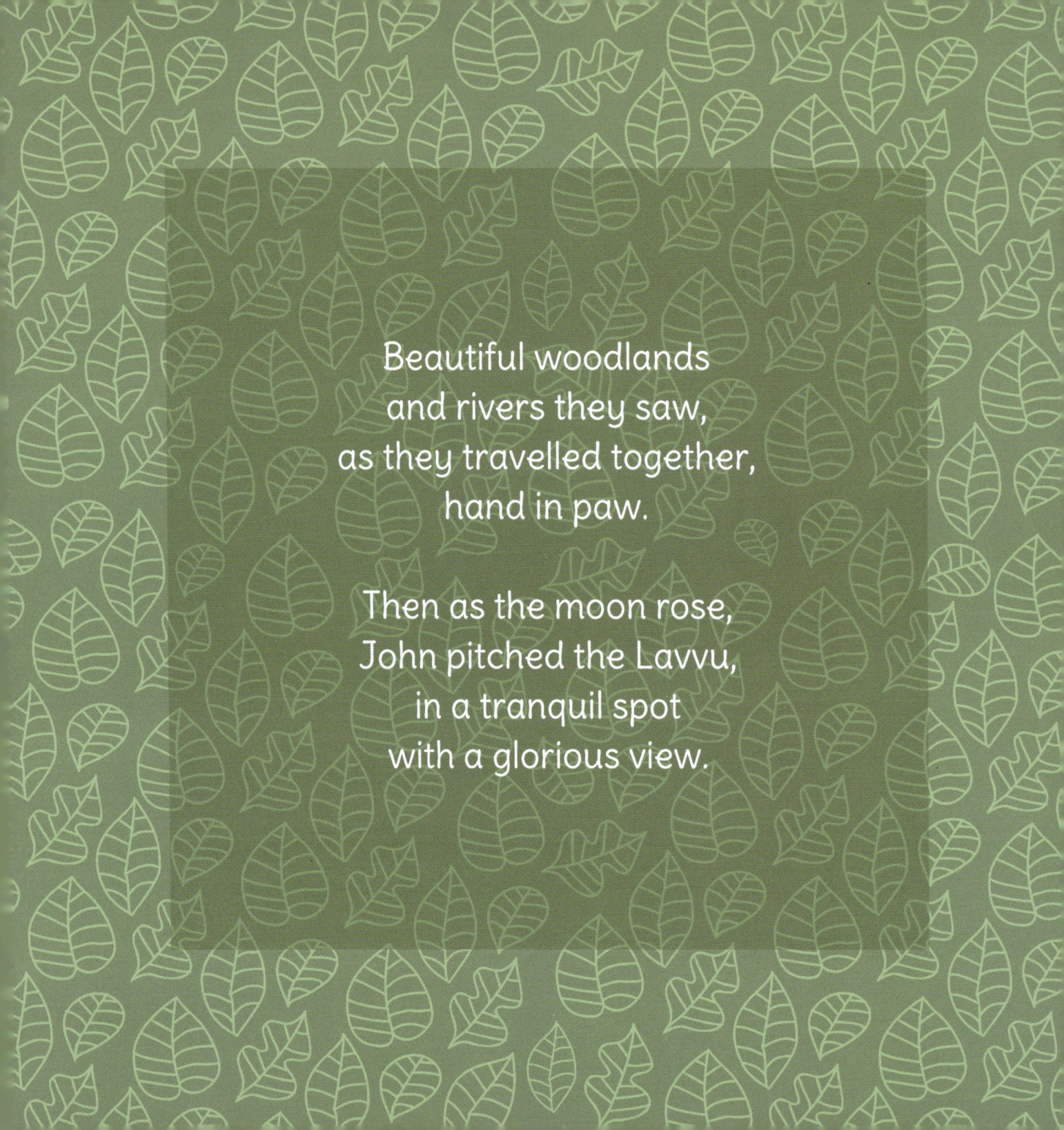

Beautiful woodlands
and rivers they saw,
as they travelled together,
hand in paw.

Then as the moon rose,
John pitched the Lavvu,
in a tranquil spot
with a glorious view.

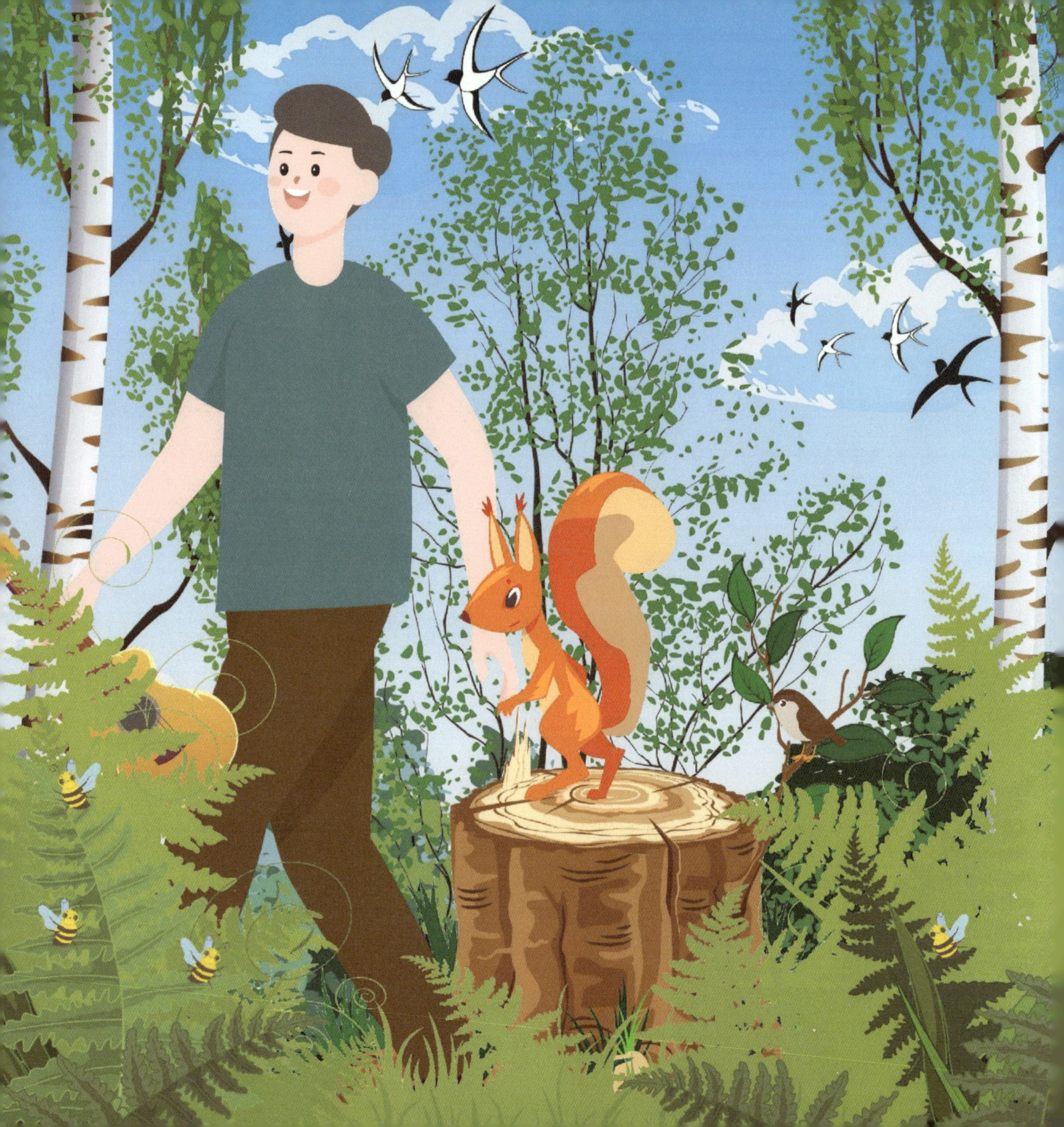

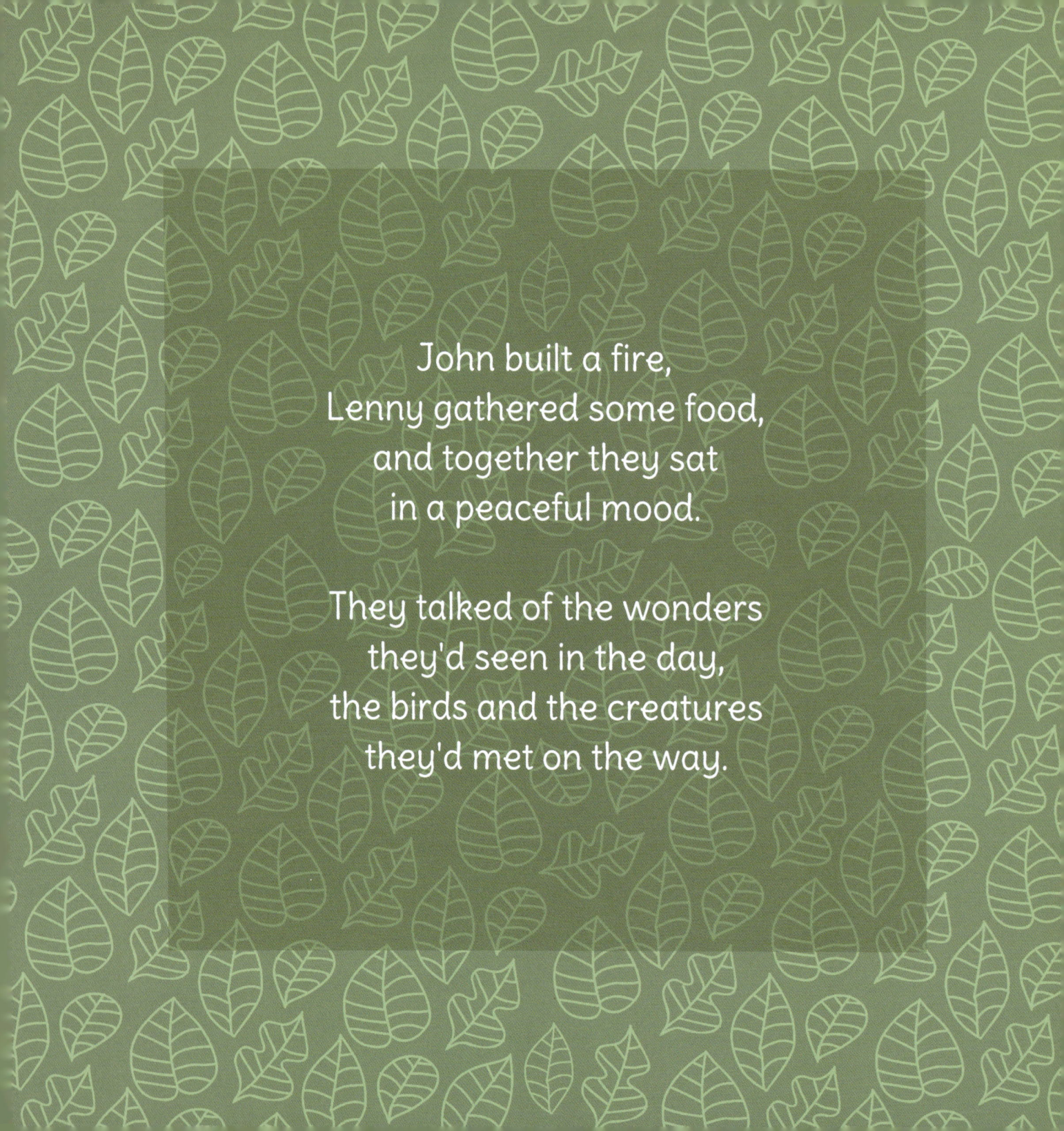

John built a fire,
Lenny gathered some food,
and together they sat
in a peaceful mood.

They talked of the wonders
they'd seen in the day,
the birds and the creatures
they'd met on the way.

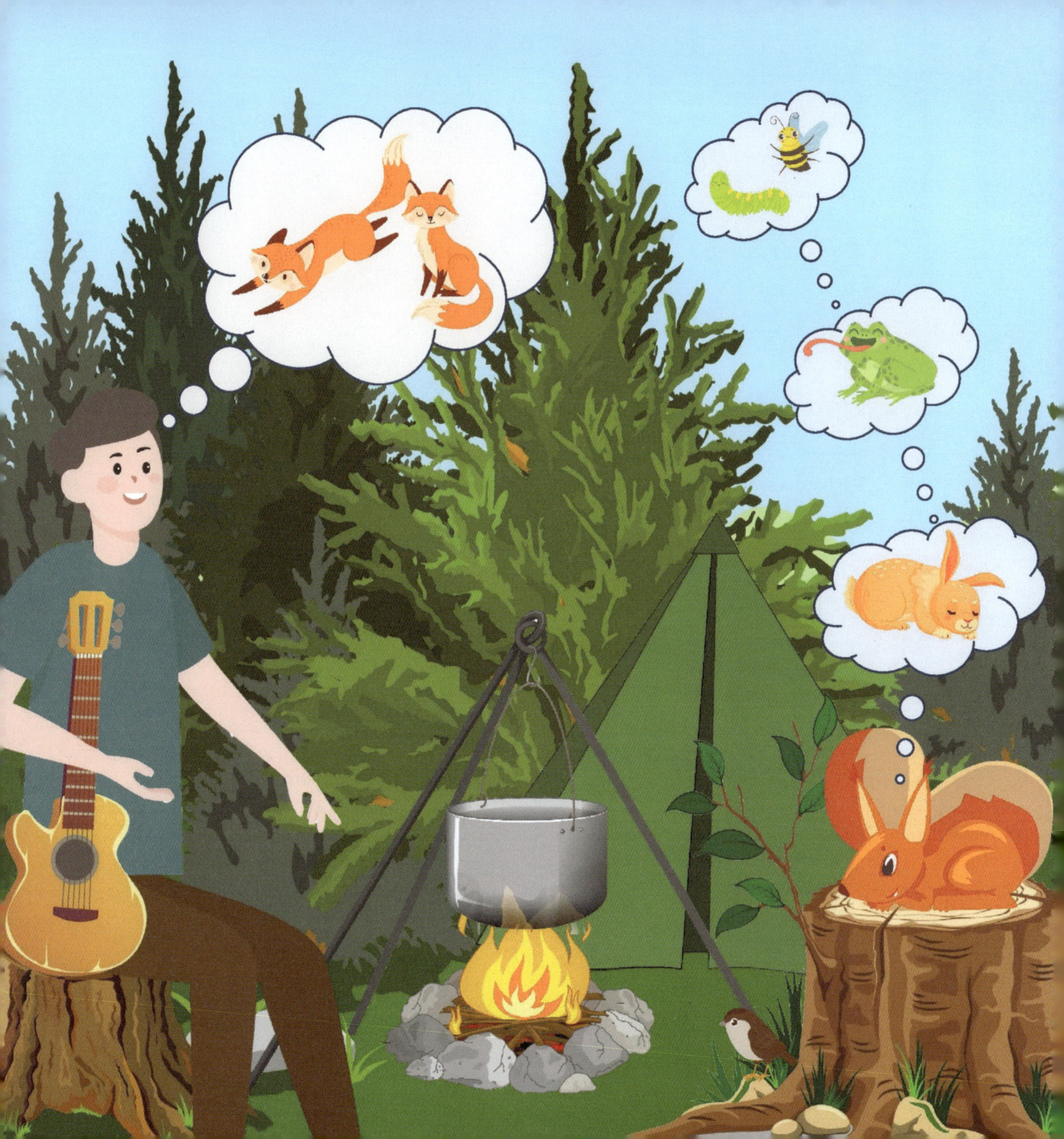

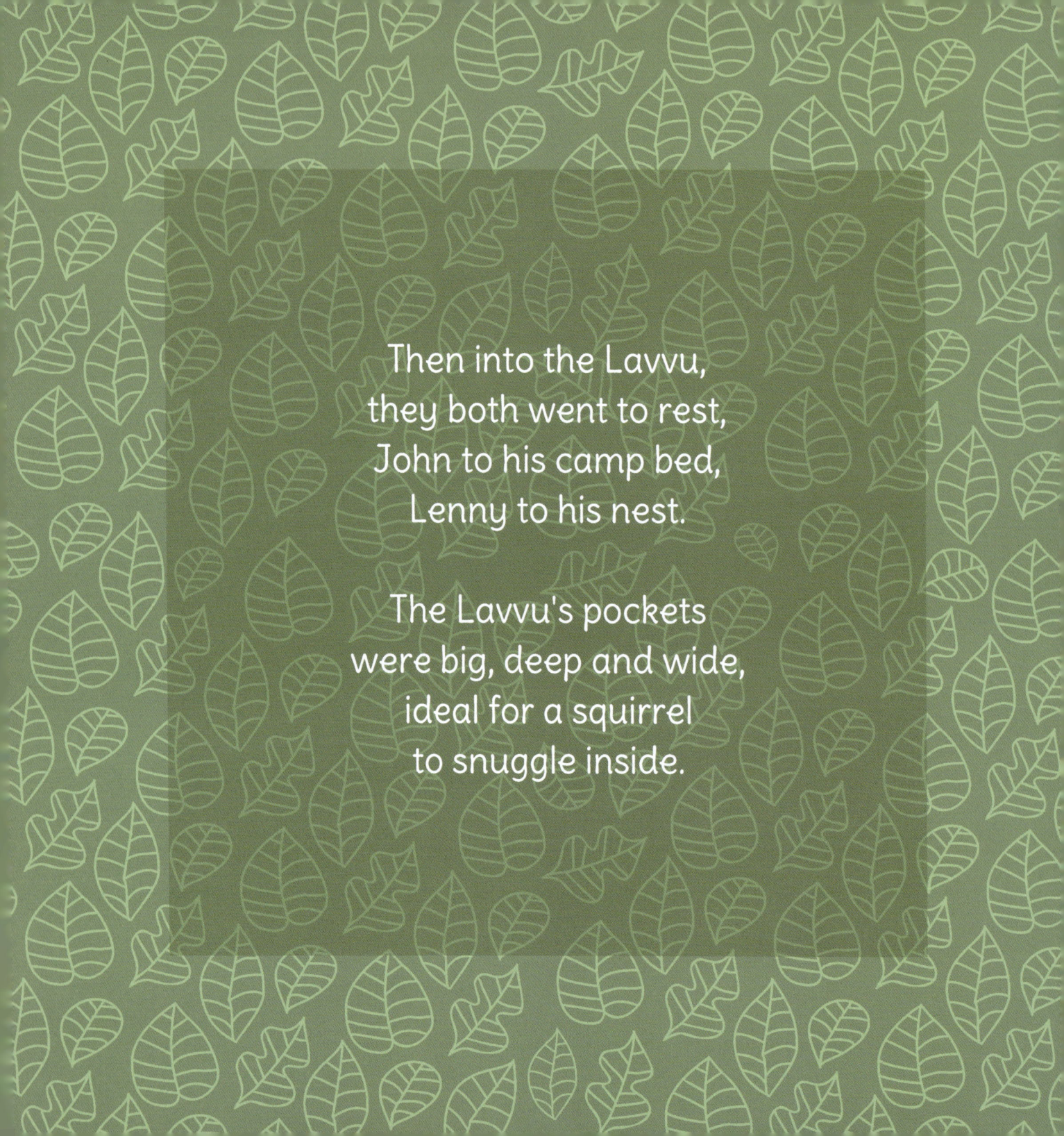

Then into the Lavvu,
they both went to rest,
John to his camp bed,
Lenny to his nest.

The Lavvu's pockets
were big, deep and wide,
ideal for a squirrel
to snuggle inside.

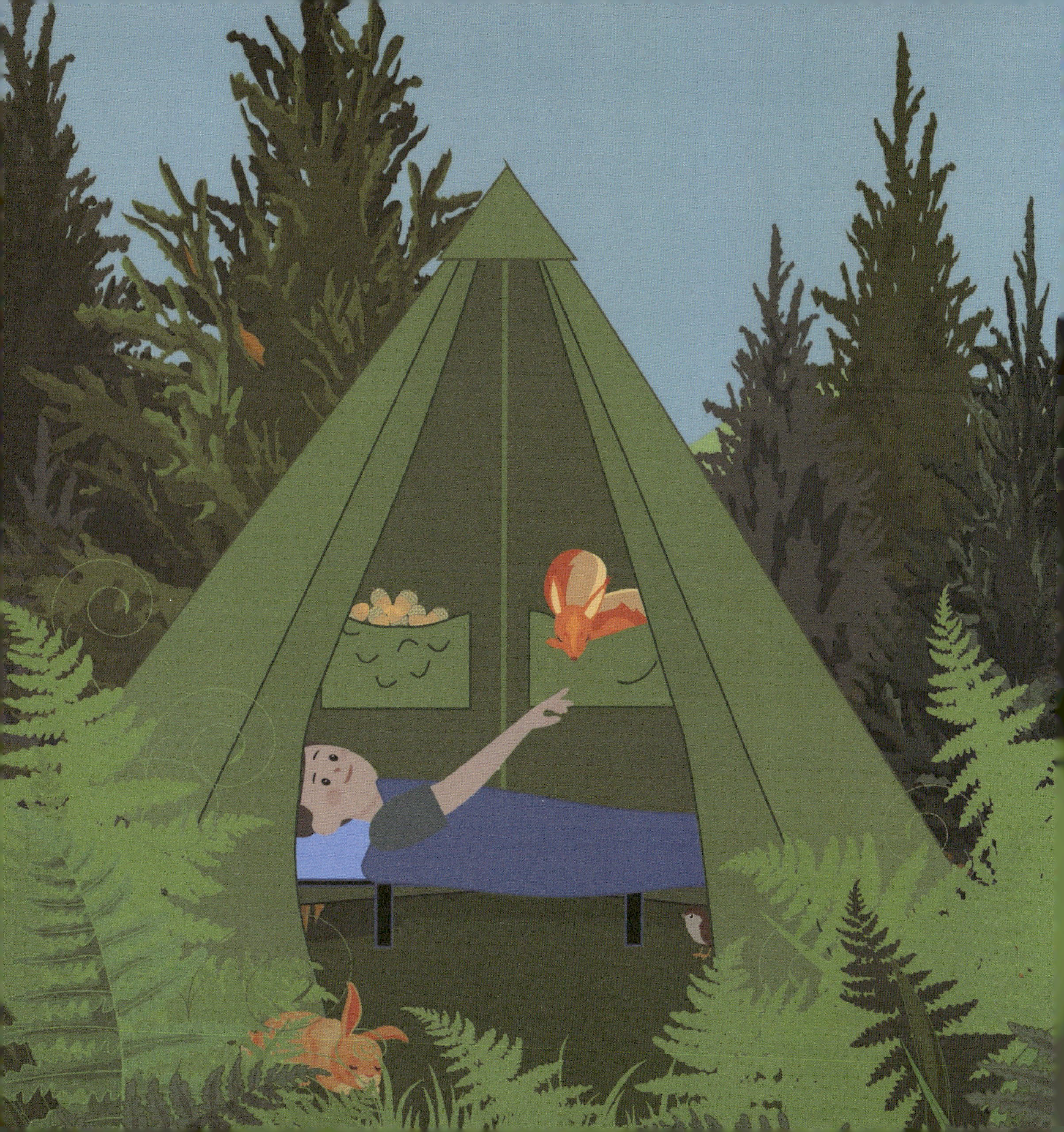

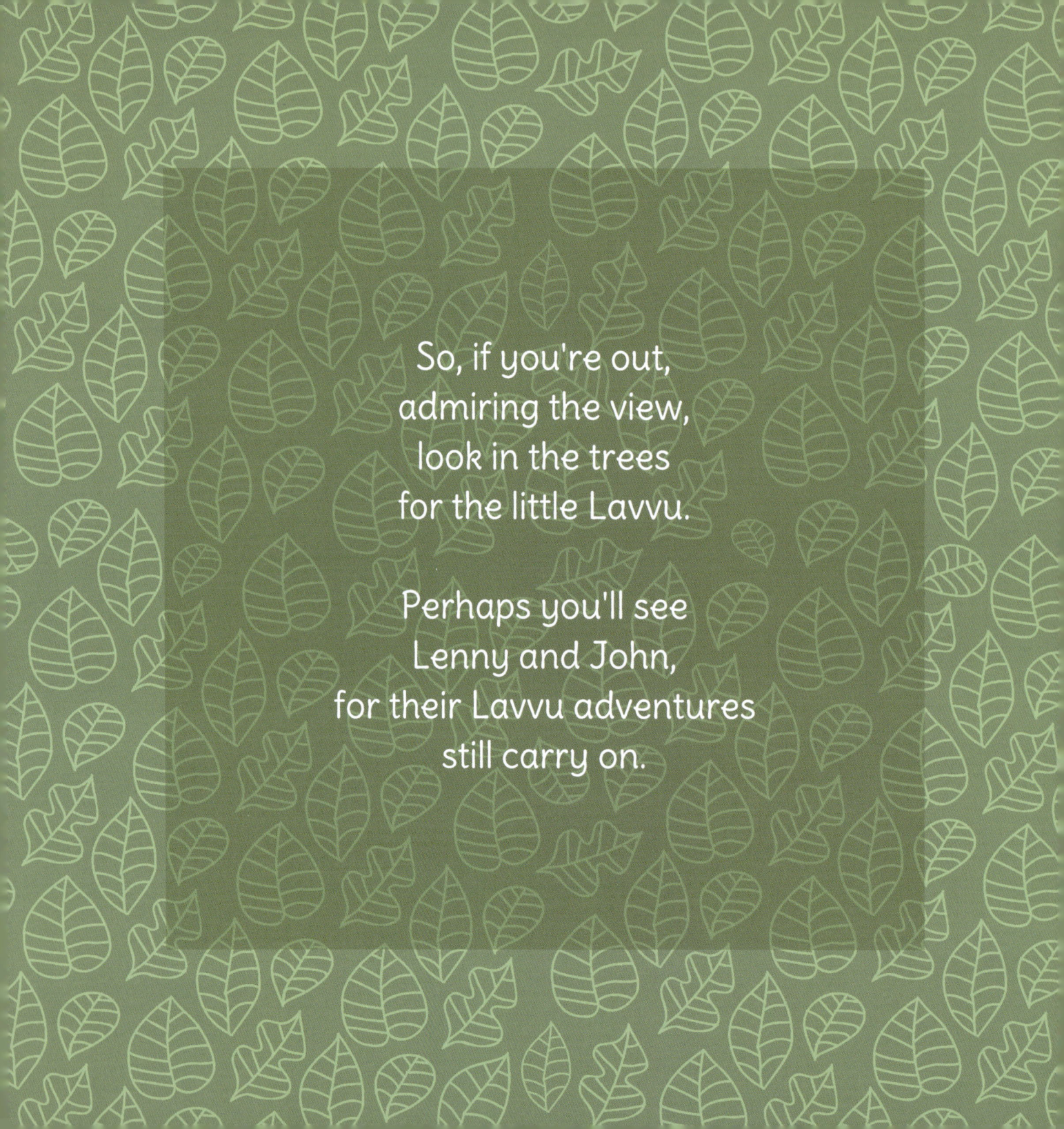

So, if you're out,
admiring the view,
look in the trees
for the little Lavvu.

Perhaps you'll see
Lenny and John,
for their Lavvu adventures
still carry on.

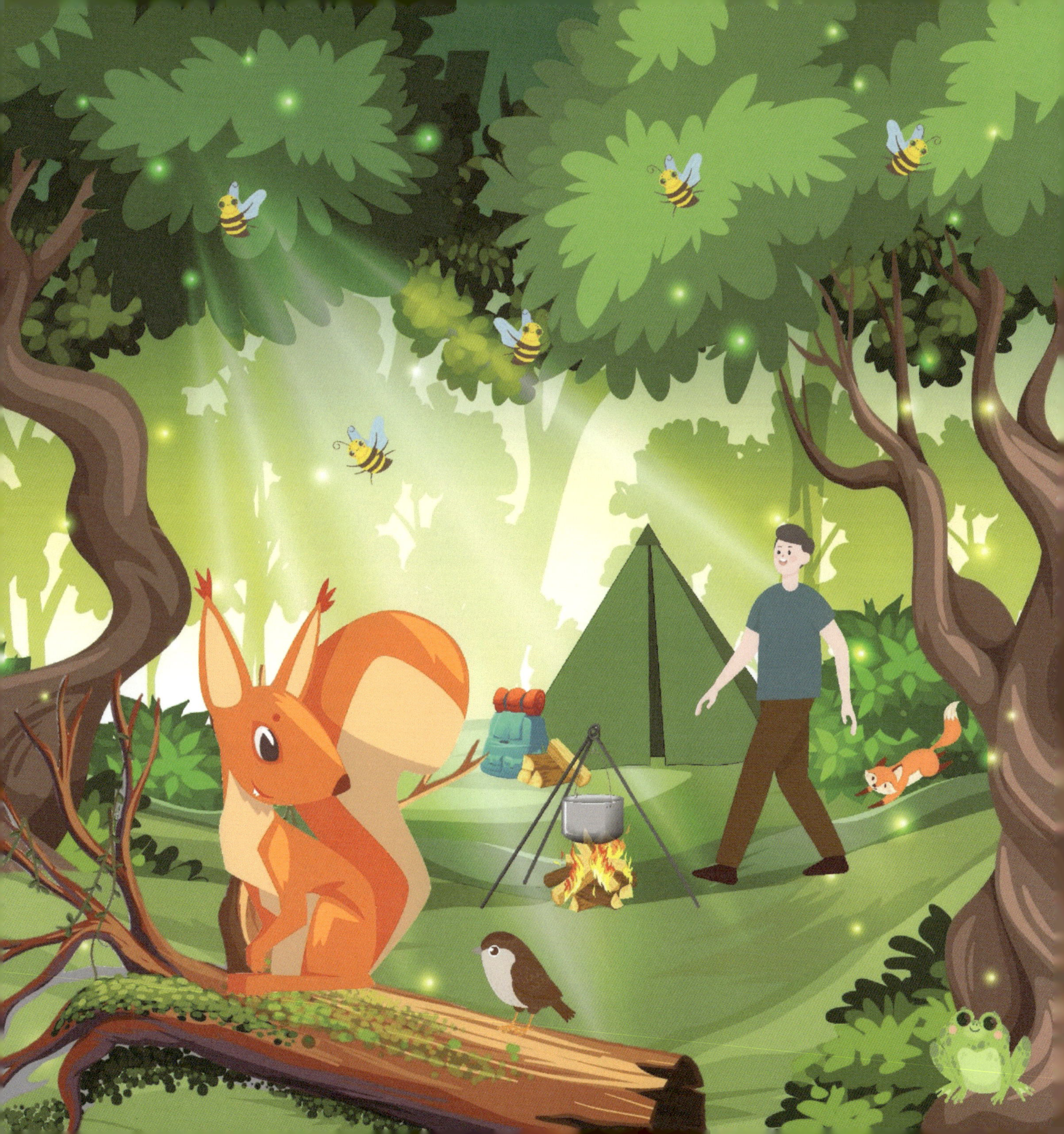

John Kelenfoldi

John is a keen Lavvu owner, and runs the biggest Lavvu group:

        Lavvu Owners Worldwide.

It's a group for likeminded people to chat about their Lavvu adventures, share their experiences and talk about anything to do with a Lavvu. If you want to join the group, search for Lavvu Owners Worldwide on Facebook, or type in the link:

https://www.facebook.com/groups/198720867439814

Sylva Fae

Sylva Fae is a married mum of three from Lancashire, England. She spent twenty plus years teaching literacy to adults with learning difficulties and disabilities, and now lives in Cheshire, juggling being a mum, writing children's stories and keeping up with the crazy antics of their naughty rabbits.

Sylva and her husband own a woodland where they enjoy camping and learning new bushcraft skills. They often go off exploring, and their woodland adventures inspired Sylva to write stories to entertain her three girls.

author.to/SylvaFae
www.facebook.com/SylvaFae
Instagram @SylvaFae

Printed in Great Britain
by Amazon